JOHN MAGUFULI
An Epitome of Cowardice

ANSBERT NGURUMO

authorHOUSE®

AuthorHouse™ UK
1663 Liberty Drive
Bloomington, IN 47403 USA
www.authorhouse.co.uk
Phone: 0800 047 8203 (Domestic TFN)
*   +44 1908 723714 (International)*

Published by AuthorHouse 06/07/2019

ISBN: 978-1-7283-8900-4 (sc)
ISBN: 978-1-7283-8901-1 (e)

DEDICATION

I dedicate this book to victims of torture in its various forms - abductions, persecutions, prosecutions, incarcerations, and extrajudicial killings; to everyone living under the shadow of fear of a dictatorship; and to everyone who cherishes and fights for democracy, human rights, and rule of law all over the world.

ACKNOWLEDGEMENT

Much as this book bears my name as author, it is a product of collective efforts of many stakeholders, particularly reliable sources of sensitive and classified information - those who collected information, narrated or scribbled it, reminded me, tipped me, and researched on issues covered in this book. It would be selfish of me as an individual to claim monopoly of knowledge or information on all these historical, cultural, behavioral, and administrative aspects as described in this book. For obvious reasons, they will remain anonymous.

Resources from the Tanzania Library Services, mainstream newspapers and online media, Controller and Auditor General's reports (2016-2018), Finance Minister's Budget Speeches (2016-2019), opposition budget speeches, interviews with businessmen, religious leaders, media leaders, members of parliament, retired civil servants, senior ruling party cadres, anonymous government officials and many others, have greatly contributed to the information analysed in this book.

Even the publishing of this book would not have been possible without financial contributions from "virtual Tanzanian friends" who, on learning that the manuscript was ready but lacking funds to publish it, made and completed donations within one week to that end. My special appreciations go to them all. Our mutual efforts have made this book OURS.

FOREWORD

Seasoned journalist Ansbert Ngurumo's new book is an important work, published at great personal risk. He was the first person – unnamed at the time – whom I heard about who was allegedly on the Magufuli government's hit list. After decades of involvement with Tanzania, I was inclined to dismiss the story as unfounded hearsay.

On a recent trip to Tanzania, a high-level European church representative told me that a Tanzanian journalist they knew had knocked on their door at 2 AM. He said he had been hunted by armed government agents and had not slept for four days. He asked if he could sleep at their house for a few hours and said he would be gone before dawn to avoid implicating them.

I also recalled hearing about the assassination attempt on Hon. Tundu Lissu, the minority whip in Parliament and then head of the Tanganyika Law Association (the Mainland bar association).

A prominent Tanzanian church leader contacted me for assistance in setting up an escape route after he was informed that his name was also on the Magufuli administration's hit list. His offense was that he, along with other high officials from several faith traditions, had openly challenged President Magufuli's suppression of the press and various extra-judicial actions against opposition politicians.

It became clear to me that these stories were all inter-connected. I do not traffic in gossip or hearsay, so I decided to talk face-to-face with all of them to verify their personal stories.

I flew to Belgium twice to meet with Hon. Tundu Lissu in the hospital where he was facing the last two of 22 major surgeries after having taken 16 bullets in his body. He and his driver, also targeted in the assassination attempt, went over the details of the attack and Lissu showed me his bullet wound and surgical scars. I also accompanied him on a recent visit to Washington, DC. I find his story entirely credible and consistent with accounts by other Tanzanian and international sources.

I talked to the Tanzanian church official both in Tanzania and abroad and several sources confirmed that he was marked for liquidation by government agents.

Finally, I decided to try to locate the unnamed journalist to verify his story. Several sources identified him as Ansbert Ngurumo, the writer of this important book. I tracked him down in one of the Nordic countries and flew there to meet with him. His story matched what I had learned on my last trip to Tanzania. He also provided a great deal of detail, which corroborated what had happened to others on the Magufuli government's hit list.

Tanzania has always been recognized for the peaceful nature of its citizens. The country has a well-deserved reputation as midwife to many of the independence movements in Africa, but equally important as a peacekeeper and mediator in the region. There is a reason why Tanzania was the site for the Rwanda War Crimes Tribunal.

Democracy depends on a free press and the freedom of political expression. President Magufuli routinely charges anyone who dares to criticize him with sedition or treason, the favored tools of autocrats and despots.

The extra-judicial killings documented in Mr. Ngurumo's book discredit the nation and its population and have impacted heavily on Tanzania's slide in the annual democracy rankings.

Julius Nyerere, Tanzania's highly respected first president, would without question have been horrified to learn what is going on under the nation's fifth government. My late father-in-law, a Sukuma like President Magufuli, would be equally horrified.

Kjell Bergh

Kjell Bergh, a Norwegian-born American citizen, has traveled to Tanzania regularly since 1974. He was married to a Tanzanian for 36 years and held investments in the Tanzania tourism sector for 20 years. Mr. Bergh was appointed Tanzania's first Honorary Consul in the United States and was Dean of all Honorary Consuls, positions he held for 15 years until he resigned when President Magufuli was elected.

INTRODUCTION

This book is not an academic presentation but a result of analysis enriched with my firsthand experience, interviews with reliable and informed sources close to the president, recommendations from high level sources, and documentary sources from the government and media. It is presented in a simple columnistic style, devoid of academic jargon, meant to give it a conversational narrative.

It is an exposure of a state of terror with which the people of Tanzania are gripped as they grapple with living in fear of each other, particularly their leaders and police. Citizens have lost their freedom and rights, as criticism and opposition are severely punished while investigations and research are highly controlled. Civic space has been shrinking since 2015 as media independence remains discouraged and stifled. Political parties can no longer hold rallies or demonstrations as they used to according to the laws of the land, and political elections are extremely militarised. Arbitrary abductions and killings are becoming the order of the day, with hundreds of citizens missing, literally killed for opposing or criticising the president. Tens of citizens have gone into exile abroad; and all that is narrated here has happened in a short span of three years.

This is a sudden change in a country previously considered one of the most peaceful, stable and secure nations in Eastern and Southern Africa. But it all boils down to one person - the president. President John Pombe Magufuli, who came to power in November 2015, has become East Africa's emerging despot whose sadistic leadership has led to numerous disappearances, ineffable tortures, abductions and killings of hundreds of civilians - mostly his critics, journalists, opposition politicians, and human rights defenders.

While some western media quickly nicknamed him "bulldozer," and one opposition politician in Tanzania called him "petty dictator," some critics have called him the "Trump of East Africa," equating his reckless, bullish and sadistic statements to those of US President Donald Trump. All this and some of his horrible actions have qualified him as a modern-day dictator on the rise. It calls for an immediate action - locally and internationally - in order to arrest the situation before it worsens and destabilizes the whole of Eastern and Southern Africa. A destabilised Africa can never augur well for the rest of the world.

In a similar manner that Italy's Benito Mussolini, Germany's Adolf Hitler, Zaire's Mobutu Sese seko and Uganda's Idi Amin rose to power and used it to crash independent thought and to crumble their countries, Magufuli has made Tanzania infamous for the wrong reasons. In just three years, Magufuli has almost successfully crashed the democratic gains of the past

27 years, replacing democracy with a one-man rule, imposing his distorted approach to leadership and development, and his disregard to democracy, human rights and rule of law.

His iron-fist rule and impulsive leadership style have led to decisions that have eventually caused dire economic conditions, closure of tens of thousands of businesses, court suits against his government, clashes between government and religious leaders, unstable relations between Tanzania and the international community - plus forcing foreign diplomats to leave the country, seeds of grand corruption and political hostility never experienced in Tanzania since independence in 1961.

Forcing everyone to fear and obey him, and attempting to make everyone toe his line and sing his praises, Magufuli is inadvertently turning his citizens into subjects. For historical, administrative and psychological reasons deeply buried within himself, he is obviously afraid of his own people and institutions - the media, parliament, Muslims, religious leaders, his party, Zanzibar and the union, the opposition, the international community, the judiciary, the business community and rich people, and others. He fears them so much that he has resolved to terrorise them as a way of silencing them and saving his face.

Throughout his political career - as a member of parliament and minister for two decades - Magufuli always behaved like a bully. Now, usurping all constitutional powers to himself as president, he has turned himself into an imperial leader with impulsive and authoritarian rule for which, in 2016, Tundu Lissu (a lawyer and Member of Parliament for Singida East) nicknamed him "a petty dictator."

During his early days as president, at least in much of 2016, Magufuli managed to fool many observers with his populist moves. Some of them quickly praised him, thinking and hoping he was going to "bulldoze" corruption and to develop Tanzania in a way never seen before. Kenyan Professor Patrice Lumumba, speaking at the University of Dar es Salaam in early 2017, went to the extreme position of wishing Africa had leaders of the calibre of John Magufuli.

In his praise, he coined the term: "Magufulification of Africa." Little did he know that *Magufulification* was going to be a new embodiment of nepotism, authoritarianism, grand corruption, diplomatic exclusionism, extrajudicial killings, abductions and tortures of civilians. Lumumba never anticipated the Magufuli that was going to bulldoze human rights in his bid to silence every critical voice. Eventually, in Magufuli's relentless attempt to put a padlock on his citizens' mouths and a noose around his critics' necks, he has become a terrifying but terrified bully; a president gripped with fear, instilling fear.

In his first three years (2015-2018), he has created a regime of terror in a befitting description by Harry S. Truman, the 33rd president of the United States of America who said: "*Once a government is committed to the principle of silencing the voice of the opposition, it has only one way to go, and that is down the path of increasingly repressive measures, until it becomes a source of terror to all its citizens and creates a country where everyone lives in fear."*

Failing to inspire and unify his people, Magufuli chose to terrorise them. Instead of motivating and accommodating his people; instead of breathing hope into their lives, he opted to intimidate them. Instead of becoming their "comforter-in-chief," he became their "terrorist-in-chief," instilling fear and insecurity instead of love and peace.

Reminiscent of past and recent dictators in many parts of Eastern Europe, South America and Africa, Magufuli has had his name inscribed on a long list of modern-day autocrats and tyrants ruling by inculcating fear. Working hard to suffocate everybody's opinion, he has apparently borrowed a leaf from the likes of the 20th century dictators. He is running his country with an iron fist, instituting the politics of cruelty and fear, terrorising everybody and, ultimately, himself.

This book offers an insider's view of this fear, in a brief analysis, explaining reasons for Magufuli's choice of fear as a leadership tool. It is my assertion that this fear is an expression of his own fearful inner self, and it is the reason for him to behave the way he does - intimidating others as he runs away from his own shadow, which he sees in the eyes of other people. In this book, I am briefly discussing 14 fears of President John Pombe Magufuli, their origin, and why it is important for Tanzania and the world to overcome them.

HIS FEAR OF BUSINESSES AND RICH PEOPLE

"Doing business in Tanzania is becoming a punishment," Hon. Jaffari Michael, MP for Moshi Urban

Although he leads a party that is ideologically socialist, Magufuli does not seem to be a socialist himself. His leadership style has proven that he follows his own impulses and ad hoc convictions about success, wealth, and poverty. Magufuli has an addictive bitterness against the business community. He has been running a government that is openly competing with and suffocating the private sector, even making it mandatory for civil servants to subscribe to the national mobile phone provider.

From his cloudy past, he had a hard time dealing with business people during his ministerial career. He harbours grudges towards those who refused to give him money or those who did not support his presidential bid. He hides his motives within his fake socialistic desires.

1

His understanding of socialism is purely anti-capital and anti-business.

Right from his early weeks in the State House, Magufuli showed his fear of successful people. In one public address in 2016, he said how he wished rich people to live like they were in hell because, in his opinion, they have been enjoying heaven on earth. In his own words, he wants them "to live like devils."

In 2018, at a public rally in Tarime, Magufuli told a crowd of listeners that the time for rich people to do whatever they wished was over, and that during his presidency, he would "do anything to them." This statement was recalled a few weeks later when some "unknown people" kidnapped Africa's youngest billionaire Mohammed Dewji in October 2018, in a saga that ended up with state security operatives being implicated.

To him, businessmen are thieves. His government has been seizing businesses of his political adversaries, prosecuting them in the pretext of fighting corruption. This position serves as his North Start - his true navigation which, in fact, is not leading him to a proper destination of actualizing his industrialization policy.

According to his close aides, Magufuli does not seek professional advice from his assistants. Instead, he demands completely religious obedience. He gives orders and directives that should not be questioned, even on matters where he lacks credible competence such as intelligence, finance, business, diplomacy, and economy. Unfortunately, when things go wrong, he blasts or fires the very people he previously forced to blindly obey him. Magufuli has an ego that keeps telling him: "When things go right, I must take credit; when they go wrong, I must blame others."

His true self is reflected in a short video clip taken months before he settled on a decision to run for president in 2015. In an informal conversation with two compatriots, one of them asks if he would vie for presidency. Immediately, as he giggles, Magufuli responds: "*Mimi? Watalimia meno*!" Literally translated, it would mean: "*Me? They will plough with their teeth.*" He clearly meant that he would give people a hard time; that he would drag people through hot coal; that people would be tortured. It is happening under his leadership.

A hand hoe is a peasant's ploughing tool for agricultural activities in most of rural Africa. Magufuli's analogy of "ploughing with teeth," makes it clear and easy for analysts to understand the origin of a high level of sadism and brutality that has manifested itself in his leadership. His statement was a prelude to his presidency of horror, cruelty and torture.

Three years on, almost every Tanzanian is "ploughing with teeth." When the billionaire was abducted in October 2018, as Tanzania's private sector struggled to endure Magufuli's personally endorsed persecution, as some investors were winding up their businesses, silently directing their capital elsewhere, translating to loss of an enormous number of jobs, and as the banking system faced the music, his statement about people "ploughing with their teeth" was slowly gaining weight.

By November 2018, the banking system was already being seriously affected, with 22 out of 45 banks facing risks of insolvency. Non-performing loans were on the rise from 6.8% in 2014 to 11.5% in 2017. A November 2018 report by the International Monetary Fund (IMF) which, among other things, notes that: "solvency stress tests have found that 22 out of Tanzania's 45 banks, representing 32% of banking assets, would become undercapitalised in the tail risk scenario. The combined effects of a sharply declining real GDP growth, rising interest rates, and depreciation of the Tanzanian Shilling reduced banks' profitability and capital ratios, mostly through their impact on credit losses and net interest income."

On the other hand, it has been confirmed by some credible circles that Magufuli creates terror as a means to seize money from rich people, particularly Tanzanians of Asian origin. Because of his unfriendly policies, his government is cash-strapped. He has played all tricks including exerting undue influence on the Bank of Tanzania to give "convenient financial reports," but he has not been capable of successfully rigging the economy in his favour.

Using his demagogic cronies and highly politicised police, he has been threatening some local tycoons with serious money laundering charges and allegedly collecting hefty portions of wealth from a good number of them, particularly those with Asian origin, with some of them invited for photo opportunities at state house. Obviously under siege, they have been speaking to the state house press unit - which circulates their video clips to all local television stations for news coverage - on the "president's great work in lifting the country's economy."

Insiders within CCM do understand that the president's move to intimidate rich business people lies in his endeavour to deter them from supporting other presidential aspirants as he works on his re-election bid for 2020. It is understood that many of those that have undergone his wrath were ardent supporters of his competitors in 2015. Some of them are implicated for supporting the opposition in the 2015 general election. He is taking reprisals while at the same time warning them against any attempt to ditch him next time.

When he became chairman of his party in 2017, he warned the party against being financed by what he termed as "dirty money" from shrewd business people. He was certainly targeting certain individuals. Surprisingly, in a sudden turn of events, when the same individuals met him and spoke on camera about the president's apparently "great work," he called them heroes and patriots. His attempt to employ the army in a forceful purchase of cashew-nuts from peasants in Mtwara region - which eventually flopped - was another expression of his distrust and fear of the business community.

Even when, because of his impulsive and autocratic style of leadership, he single-handedly picked a Kenyan company and granted it a lucrative contract worth $180 million for the purchase of 100,000 tonnes of cashew-nuts from Tanzania, it emerged almost immediately that the Magufuli government had been conned. His government ignored warnings from media, parliamentarians and experts. His former PhD supervisor, working as permanent secretary for trade and industries,

Prof. Joseph Buchweishaja, defended the government move and the credibility of the company. But within two months, it turned out that the Kenyan company lacked financial ability, competence, and business record to purchase cashew-nuts.

The army messed up and failed to purchase cashew-nuts. Instead, soldiers terrified peasants and local traders, and confiscated some of their produce. The government embarrassingly disappointed peasants and itself. And the peasants lost money and cashew-nuts. According to veteran journalist and lawyer Jenerali Ulimwengu, the cashew-nuts flop was an economic sabotage by authorities. Cashew-nut peasants are not the only victims of Magufuli's controlled economy. Between 2015 and 2019, the price of coffee in some cooperative societies in Tanzania has fallen from 2,200 shillings (about $1) to 800 shillings (less than $0.5) per kilo.

As the Magufuli government becomes a chief (and almost the only) player in investing and running business, it becomes obvious that his economic approach highly discourages growth of the private sector in Tanzania. As his government attempts to compete with investors and business people, it becomes clear that he wants them to "plough with their teeth" and kneel before the government; and his only way to actualise that is to suffocate their businesses.

HIS FEAR OF HIS OWN PARTY

"Had I been the chairman, on that very day, more than a quarter or half of them would have perished," President John Magufuli, referring to those in his party who had not been happy with his nomination as presidential candidate.

As a matter of fact, very few of his party members or his country men and women expected Magufuli to run for president. Even when he did, not many expected him to win. The secret of his victory lied within a very small circle of party elders - Ali Hassan Mwinyi (former president), Benjamin William Mkapa (former president), Salmin Amour (former president), Amani Karume (former Zanzibar president), John Malecela (former prime minister and vice-president), Cleopa Msuya (former prime minister) and Pius Msekwa (former speaker for the national assembly).

Msekwa worked as secretary to this elders' council to determine who their party would eventually nominate as a presidential candidate for the 2015 elections. Then sitting president Jakaya Kikwete, was briefed on the elders' unanimous decision, and it was his duty as party chairman to team up with his secretary general Abdulrahman Kinana in influencing the nomination process with the help of the security system.

As it has always been in Tanzania, once this council has made a decision and the president has endorsed it, the general election is over. The campaigns and voting process are merely meant to justify the ruling party's choice of president. The elders' decision influences all other organs of the party, particularly the Central Committee - whose wish is automatically passed by the national executive committee and the general congress.

Come what may, the elders' choice must win the nomination and the final battle. But narratives on how Magufuli made it in 2015 differ. While some sources within CCM say he was the elders' choice imposed on the sitting president, others say he was an accidental compromise of warring factions within the ruling party.

One narrative that seems to hold weight says that the elders settled on two extreme choices, Bernard Membe and John Magufuli. Politically, Membe (then foreign minister) was stronger. The party elders had grappled with two factors - stopping Edward Lowassa (former prime minister) from contesting, and nominating a Christian candidate. They wanted to maintain their long-held culture within the party of alternating between Muslim and Christian presidents.

So, even though the top five candidates included three Muslims - January Makamba, Asha-Rose Migiro, and Amina Salum Ali - it was certain that the party's choice for candidate was going to be between Membe and Magufuli. And because the Central Committee had ditched one of the strongest and most popular candidates, Lowassa, whose main competitor within CCM was Membe, and Lowassa's supporters had come with a conclusion that President Kikwete's choice was Membe, they plotted to make the best revenge by voting him (Membe) out in the National Executive Committee (NEC). Membe's supporters, however, blamed Kikwete for not standing by their candidate.

That was how the NEC sent three names - Amina Salum Ali, Asha-Rose Migiro, and John Magufuli - to the National Congress for a final nomination vote. And that was how Magufuli eventually emerged a CCM flag bearer.

There is another way of looking at his path to nomination. His party was facing a very stiff opposition from the public for two main reasons. Firstly, accused of harbouring grand corruption, and facing stiff opposition, it feared being ousted from power. It had to find a way not to relinquish it.

Secondly, some progressive minds within CCM were well aware of the fact that some people within were proposing some fundamental changes as a way of rejuvenating the party that had overstayed in power. It was obviously difficult for the party to choose a new president who had deep roots in the ruling party, as he would definitely not accept some proposals for vital changes, especially if he feared that such changes would negatively affect some of his comrades or himself.

So, as a matter of principle, the elders sought for someone with little or no allegiances within the party; someone who would have nothing to lose in shylessly taking hard decisions that would shape both the party and the country. Their analysis showed that, people of this calibre within CCM, according to some sources, included Magufuli and former energy minister Sospeter Muhongo. When Muhongo was fired in the midst of corruption allegations involving an escrow account between the government and the Independent Power Tanzania Limited (IPTL), a way was certainly paved for Magufuli.

But it was not an easy ride for him. He was not a popular candidate in his party. He did not command respect in the party ranks. To many, Magufuli looked like a stranger because, despite having been a member of parliament and minister since 1995, he had never held any party post at any level.

So, party members suspected his political prowess and leadership skills. His competitors despised him because he did not command any meaningful following. Those who knew his health problems ascertained themselves that he would never pass the first screening test. Surprisingly, and against all odds, the weakest contender made through to the final. Some rules were bent to make this happen; and this move exasperated many CCM stalwarts and cadres.

As per CCM constitution, every aspirant seeking nomination for presidential candidate must seek a specified minimum number of signatures set by the party from its members in all 30 regions within a given period.

Magufuli went through a hard time obtaining signatures from members in many regions. He later complained that at some point, because of his unpopularity, some party members risked asking him to offer something in exchange for their signatures, while some of his competitors - particularly Edward Lowassa, Bernard Membe and January Makamba - had thousands of members following them, freely offering their signatures.

Magufuli had to endure this embarrassing process until the final day of his nomination. The most influential aspirants were removed from the race without proper explanation, automatically paving way for him. And although President Kikwete bravely shouldered the blame for allegedly ditching his former right hand man and prime minister Lowassa, and one of his preferences, Membe, he has on several accounts told some of his confidants that, "my hands are clean on Magufuli nomination." He blames Lowassa's angry supporters for having voted in a pattern that eventually paved a way for Magufuli.

So, it was a surprise to many for Magufuli to emerge among the top five from a group of 42 aspirants, and later among the top three that made it to the general congress. In their party's history no one has ever been nominated presidential candidate who had never been a party insider. As a socialist party with a communist-oriented culture and inclination, CCM was expected to nominate a candidate who had once been a member of its central committee.

For this reason, Magufuli's nomination was a surprise to him too. Whether it was the president or the elders' council that wanted him, for CCM, Magufuli became a compromise choice between Lowassa and Membe.

But the CCM's decision to ditch Lowassa never went without causing havoc within the party. With the strongest contenders left out, some angry supporters - including senior members and leaders - spoke to the media against President Kikwete's "undemocratic action." Some of them threatened to quit the party. Others quit at a later stage.

Even though Lowassa's supporters switched allegiance to Amina Salum Ali, seeking to "punish" President Kikwete for striking out their choice, it never worked in their favour because it was not their vote that counted but the elders and the president's choice. Some sources within CCM claim that Amina won the nomination vote on July 12, 2015, but victory was rigged in favour of the president's accidental choice - Magufuli. Security agents were employed to silence Amina and to quel grumbling members, the voters. And, due to this controversy (of who actually won the nomination), it took over 12 hours for the results to be released.

Surprisingly though, as the members sat in the hall waiting for President Kikwete and his team to resume and announce the results, another surprise awaited both Kikwete and Magufuli. As the president stepped in the conference hall, a huge section of members started clapping and chanting in unison: "Tuna imani na Lowassa, oya oya oya..." They meant that they had trust in Lowassa!

After a minute or so, the president and his assistants discovered they had been clapping for wrong music. They stopped, but the message of the song was an obvious ridicule to the president (chairman) and the party. It was the same tune they have always used in previous elections by asserting their allegiance and confidence to the nominated candidate. But the wording was seriously troubling.

In 1995, after a similar process, the members burst into singing, "tuna imani na Mkapa, oya oya oya..." meaning, "we trust Mkapa, oya oya oya..." In 2015, at Kikwete's nomination, they sang again, "tuna imani na Kikwete, oya oya oya..." This time, even before the nominated candidate was declared, and while knowing that the winner must be either Amina or Magufuli or Asha, a huge section of properly organised CCM national congress members sang in unison: "Tuna imani na Lowassa, oya oya oya..!" Yet Lowassa was not on the ballot. That was an embarrassment to President Kikwete and it was a clear message to him and the nominated candidate that the party was divided, and a good chunk of it was obviously against the president's choice, Magufuli.

It was no surprise, therefore, that when Lowassa later crossed over to the opposition and became a presidential candidate to challenge Magufuli, it became obvious that CCM, the only party that has ruled Tanzania for five decades, was facing an uphill battle, on the verge of losing power. Their only consolation lied in the fact that they had support from the Tanzania Intelligence and Security Services (TISS) which, in worst case scenario, would ultimately influence a final decision of the National Electoral Commission - which is also under the president's office.

CCM insiders understand that Magufuli garnered not more than 45 percent of the general election vote but, through insidious influences that aimed at deterring the opposition from taking power, he was declared winner with 58.46 percent of the vote - the lowest ever for a CCM presidential candidate.

His predecessors had scored higher. In 1995, Mkapa was declared winner with 61.8 percent, while Kikwete won the 2005 election with 80.28 percent. Even after the results were officially announced, there was no jubilations of the level and kind expected of a winning party. The country was in shock and panic. But that was it. The constitution of Tanzania does not give room to anyone to challenge presidential results in any way. That way, Magufuli found himself in state house without a clear support of his party. He feared them, and they did not trust him.

When some of his assistants eventually confided to him the secret of his presidential victory, he even feared and disliked them more. He designed a secret strategy to distance himself from them because he would not feel confident working with and commanding people who, he thought, knew the party and the system more than he did. He fired them one after another in a bid to create his new and obedient inner circle. This revelation and feeling affected his confidence as he kept insisting, in many of his public speeches, that "whether you like it or not, your president is John Pombe Magufuli." In a way, he was projecting his deeply buried hatred against the voters for not giving him enough votes in 2015, and his fear of those who assisted him to "win" the election.

Moreover, as a new president and later as chairman of CCM, Magufuli nursed anger and reprisals against certain personalities in his own party because of the way he had been treated during his nomination process and during the election campaigns. When Kikwete called the party national congress to endorse Magufuli as a new chairman on July 23, 2017, Magufuli publicly made a reference to one unhappy moment he had experienced on his nomination day in 2015.

Referring to President Kikwete and thanking him for standing by him at the most trying moment when the party almost rejected him, Magufuli said: "He trusted me and made sure I sailed through all party procedures and nomination process..."

Then he told his predecessor: "I thank you. You have suffered a lot of derision and insults for my sake.. With love and trust in God, you kept quiet... You are a peculiar person, with a sense of patience that I do not happen to possess. Sincerely speaking, on that (my nomination) day, as you re-entered a conference hall and found members chanting in unison that they had trust in someone else (Lowassa) ... Had I been the chairman, on that very day, more than a quarter or half of them would have perished. I still try to consult my heart... I do not know what would have happened if I had been in the same position and situation as you."

When he uttered these words, some CCM congress members in the hall took it for humor. They clapped and cheered for him. They did not realise that it was brewing to their own detriment. While they seemed to be concentrating on his apparent joke - that wasn't a joke at all - he was contemplating how to take reprisals against those who never supported him - in fact, some of the cheering members.

As a witty stranger in the party leadership, he had to start with appointments that were going to shake the party leadership, as he constructed his own base, recruiting his cronies and intelligence operatives to replace party insiders. That was the only way he would control and run the party as he wishes, using presidential powers and security agents to impose agenda in its secretariat, and in the party caucus to determine important parliamentary decisions.

Against this background, Magufuli still looks uncertain in his position as president. He is aware that his presidency has caused more misery than prosperity to the citizens and to his own party. He gets regular briefs on grumbles from disgruntled members and leaders. He is aware of his low approval rates, and he fears anyone who would wish to challenge him in the 2020 election. On a fair and level play field, Magufuli cannot expect to get an automatic nomination for reelection.

As a strategy to keep everyone at par, he is terrorising his own people in a number of ways, including planting surrogates working to tarnish names of his potential competitors and their supporters within his party. He is already targeting two former ministers and one cabinet minister.

Even when Africa's youngest billionaire, Mohammed Dewji, was kidnapped in October 2018 in a way that partly implicated the security system and some of his cronies, word went out that the businessman was not in the good books of the "big man" because of his close allegiance to some of the president's former challengers.

Gripped with fear, Magufuli is attempting to instil the same fear in his own party as a way of obtaining full power and total obedience from people who understand the party intrigues more than he does. Surprisingly, he is attempting to terrorise even his predecessors whenever he feels they may come out to say something in a way that would openly criticise his administration and sway masses.

On different occasions, two of his predecessors had to wait for continental forums outside Tanzania to speak up, albeit indirectly, against his leadership style. Without mentioning names, he once sent a strong message by warning "some retired leaders who have a tingling to speak up" against his administration.

Although he has said on several occasions that he was not so much into the presidency, his behaviour shows he is attempting to have a very tight grip on the presidency to the extent of threatening his potential competitors. A year before the 2020 general elections, there is every indication that he is already campaigning, with his cronies threatening and mudslinging some possible heavy weights in his party considered to be wishing to run for president in 2020.

There are fears within CCM that if Magufuli wins nomination and election for a second term in 2020, he may end up changing the constitution to give himself a longer term in the same way Rwanda's Paul Kagame and Uganda's Yoweri Museveni did. His party does not wish this to happen. What will they do? No one knows.

All in all, anybody's way to the presidency, as it stands now, lies not in the hands of the party or the voters. It all rests in the discretion of the CCM elders' council and security agents who deal with intra-party politics and the electoral commission to influence results. That is how it is easy in Tanzania for someone to win or lose a smoothly and properly staged sham general election, expensively funded.

HIS FEAR OF MEDIA

"I would like to tell media owners - be careful, watch it. If you think you have that kind of freedom, not to that extent," President John Magufuli, warning media against criticising him and his government.

His efforts to suffocate media have somehow paid off because, in the past three years since 2016, media in Tanzania have become almost irrelevant. Due to government over censorship, media do not offer any substantive news. They do not do any serious investigation. They have lost a nose for useful tips and beautiful angles. They have lost their watchdog role. If anything, against their own policies, they have turned into Magufuli's lapdogs.

Usually, the government is the main advertiser, using media to reach its prospective audience. Under Magufuli, the government has been using advertisements as a carrot in a way to corrupt some media, and as a stick to punish those that want to retain their professional line by doing authentic journalism. Overall, media revenues have been curtailed due to the government's selective allocation of advertisements, as well as increased threats to publishers, editors and printers.

With hefty taxes imposed on them, like any other businesses, they all are forced to toe the line. As it stands, many media companies have literally no financial capacity to pay salaries for up to 12 months. Angry reporters and editors cannot avoid being corrupted. Some media houses are likely to close down business in the near future.

The trend shows that the Magufuli government is funding media sycophants created by and for the regime to publish propaganda and sing vain praises of his "successes." Such media have the least reach in terms of circulation, but they get the lion's share of government adverts. Unfortunately, professionalism has been overshadowed by cheerleading.

A few instances may serve as clear examples of Magufuli's initiatives to muzzle media. In 2016, some of Magufuli's aides leaked information that he was determined to close down critical media outlets owned by Hali Halisi Publishers Limited, whose two directors happen to be opposition members of parliament. By September 2017 the government had successfully muzzled the three targeted newspapers - Mawio, Mseto and MwanaHALISI. Two of their editors were arraigned in court accused of sedition. Their consulting managing editor - this author - had a narrow shave, and luckily fled from abductors into exile for his life.

For 10 years that preceded Magufuli's presidency, the media used to broadcast live all parliamentary sessions. It had helped citizens to follow parliamentary debates and assess the performance of their representatives in parliament. But it was obvious that this live session immensely embarrassed the government and the ruling party because, in many instances, corruption scandals were unveiled and debated through parliament. It exposed the government and gave credit to the opposition.

Magufuli ordered this live programme scrapped off within his first few months in power. Instead, he instituted a live coverage of events in which he is involved. He enjoys live media coverage wherever he goes. Most of video clips concerning him are recorded by the state house media unit, then distributed to other televisions stations - interfering with, and controlling, editorial independence of private media.

Between 2010 and 2015 my colleagues and I used to organise and broadcast a popular TV show, "The Tanzania We Want," alternating between two national TV stations - Star Tv and ITV. Hosted by Rosemary Mwakitwange, the programme gave citizens an opportunity to discuss and raise direct questions on major issues of national interest by engaging the program guests. After Magufuli's installation as president, I went to one these TV station in 2016, seeking to revive the show.

On learning that I wanted to do public debates that would provide deep analysis on socio-political matters, despite the fact that we used to pay the station handsomely, the editor openly told me, "I am afraid, we won't be able to run this programme because the president will not like it." I was astonished. But that was it. Silently, Magufuli was slowly and silently instituting himself as the defacto editor-in-chief of many media outlets.

In November 2016, working to lure public approval on the day the parliament was supposed to pass or ditch the highly contentious Media Services Act that was opposed by media stakeholders, the State House organised a press conference for the president. It involved specially selected journalists and, for propaganda purposes, it was broadcast live.

One seasoned journalist, Paschal Mayala, asked the president the toughest question of the day. He wanted Magufuli to tell Tanzanians where from he had obtained exclusive powers to criminalise and ban public rallies and demonstrations, while such activities were provided for in the constitution. Magufuli never responded to that question. Instead, he cracked a joke about the meaning of the journalist's surname in his local language - Kisukuma. He said Mayala means "famine or hunger."

At that moment, few or none construed what Magufuli implied by this response. Apparently, Majura had been working for years as media consultant to the government's various units. Weeks after his question to Magufuli, he received letters, one after another, from the government units he has been working with, each bearing bad news. Most of them were either revoking their working contracts with him or expressing intent of not renewing the contracts with him in the following cycle. The message was clear. They had been ordered to let him go jobless and hungry - just like his name suggests!

In March 2017, Magufuli made yet another strong statement at state house during a swearing in ceremony of a new information minister, Dr. Harrison Mwakyembe. It was broadcast live. Speaking in Kiswahili mixed with broken English, Magufuli warned media owners on the limit of press freedom. He said: "I would like to tell media owners - be careful, watch it. If you think you have that kind of freedom, not to that extent." He meant "watch out!"

Since then, the media in Tanzania have suffered the consequences of being professional, investigative, analytical and critical. Besides the laws, severe regulations have been written to limit freedom of the press. For the first time in history, bloggers have to be approved by the government and then apply for a licence for which they pay a huge sum of money.

Researchers - media or academic or otherwise - are not allowed to publish data not approved by, or obtained from, his government. An organisation that released poll results showing Magufuli's popularity sharply dwindling faced the music. Its director's passport was seized. His citizenship was questioned.

Unfortunately, not much of this made headlines great enough to attract international attention until security operatives posing as immigration police arrested two foreign journalists working with the Committee to Protect Journalists (CPJ), Angela Quintal and Muthoki Mumo, who had been on a professional tour of Tanzania in November 2018. They were badly treated, their passports temporarily confiscated, then released after a global uproar on their arrest. In her narrative after their release and unhappy departure, Quintal wrote in South Africa's *Daily Maverick*:

"While we could fly out of Dar, we remain concerned that the journalists we left behind did not have the luxury of doing the same. We fear they will be targeted when the furore dies down and that the suppression of the Tanzanian press will escalate in the lead-up to the 2020 election. Local journalists deserve the same support and solidarity that Muthoki and I received. Yet if there is a silver lining, it is that many people the world over have finally woken up to Magufuli's repression. Pressure must be stepped up to allow a free and diverse press to flourish and for the government to finally come clean about the fate of Azory Gwanda."

Gwanda, a journalist with *Mwananchi* newspaper, was abducted on November 21, 2017. Despite calls from media stakeholders and other human rights activists, there has been no trace of him since. In April 2019, the information minister spoke up in parliament threatening to take action against anyone questioning the disappearance of the journalist. It is understood that Gwanda was abducted at a time he was doing an investigation on extra judicial killings in Kibiti district where hundreds of people had been arbitrary killed by police.

Some civilians, in efforts to save themselves or take reprisals, had also killed some police officers. The government did not, and still does not, want anyone to question or follow up on the Kibiti killings. Obviously, Magufuli and his government have no explanation; and they are to blame for fearing their people so much as to kill them.

Magufuli has put a tight noose on the media because he fears the impact of free and independent media. He has been personally calling and warning editors against critical coverage of his government or himself. He enjoys it only when he is not targeted, and when he wants to use the same media to expose certain people before taking action against them.

As a result of Magufuli's fear of media and his efforts to muzzle their freedom and independence, the 2019 press freedom index by Reporters Without Borders put Tanzania on number 118 out of 180 countries covered. This is a slip of 25 points from its previous position at 93 in 2018, and a serious drop of 49 points from its 69th position five years ago (2014).

In one of the articles describing my ordeal, published by South Africa's *Mail & Guardian Online* in March 2018, I wrote:

In early 2016, when Magufuli sent a friend to warn me about my writings, I was not overly alarmed. "The big man is asking, what did he wrong you that makes you keep hammering him in your articles?" his envoy asked me. But I kept voicing my concerns, particularly in my 15-year-old column, Maswali Magumu, Swahili for "tough questions", about his autocratic endeavour to muzzle freedom of expression. I never envisaged this catastrophe. As it stands now, the shrinking space for freedom of expression threatens progress and puts the country's security at risk. It paves the way for grand corruption.

What is happening in Tanzania under Magufuli, perfectly fits into what I predicted in my other article published by *The East African* newspaper on December 19, 2016 with a headline: "*Critical minds in Tanzania have a hard time with Magufuli.*" Following this article, the government's spokesperson doubling as the registrar of newspapers, reprimanded the newspaper editor saying he should not have published my article. The editor stood by his position and gave the government a space in the next issue to have its opinion heard instead of choosing for him what to publish. I was later informed that the newspaper was eventually warned against publishing my articles.

In mid May 2019, the management of New Habari (2006) temporarily suspended their daily newspaper - MTANZANIA - citing technological and management reasons, but insiders understood well that the decision had been imposed by state house following a cartoon that displayed Magufuli and Makonda in a way the president did not like. He called the owner and addressed the matter with him. Apparently, this owner, - Magufuli's recent business complicit - promised him to deal with the matter in a way that would neither embarrass him nor expose the government. He "banned" his own newspaper for one month to please Magufuli. The ban, however, was lifted after a week, but the cartoonist, Said Michael, was completely banned from offering his services to the newspaper.

It is an open secret that he has planted informers in every newsroom. Some of them are senior reporters and editors. They silently monitor fellow journalists on the type of news tips they generate, the story angles they choose, and personal comments they make about the president. Bent on getting rid of critical reporting about his government, Magufuli has been colluding with, or advising, some media owners to either reshuffle or fire uncompromising editors. In some cases, he personally calls and reprimands editors.

Magufuli never believes in the power of independent media in transforming the country because he never believes that freedom, democracy and development go hand in hand. He abhors serious investigative media because he fears they will uncover hidden grand corruption in his "clean" government. He never believes in freedom of expression because he is a natural despot. He terrorises media because he fears them, and he uses them for his cheap propaganda. He fears the media because he knows their power, and he wishes to rule over an ignorant and uninformed citizenry. He fears media because he has much to hide from them. And he knows that the only way to keep them at bay, at least temporarily, is by suffocating and terrorising them.

HIS FEAR OF THE OPPOSITION

"His party rigged the last general election for him.... He is restricting political and civil freedom to deter us from organising the people's power. But with strategies, intelligence and integrity the opposition will prevail beyond his fears," Hon. John Mnyika, MP for Kibamba, Dar es Salaam

Magufuli's fear and dislike of opposition probably dates back to 1985 when, as a political novice, he contested for the first time and lost to Phares Kabuye in a parliamentary election for Biharamulo constituency. He lost to him again in 1990. In all parliamentary elections that he took part after that, Magufuli always developed a political manoeuvre that would either let him go unopposed or give him the weakest challenger within his party. He is notoriously known for corrupting or threatening or having his competitor temporarily detained for him to go unopposed. When it involves him contesting with others, Magufuli is known as rough player and a ruthless bully.

Within three months of his presidency, on February 5, 2016, at his party's 39th anniversary celebrated in Singida region, Magufuli made a speech, broadcast live, in which he expressed his fears and dislike of competitive politics.

He said he would obliterate the opposition before the 2020 general elections because, to him, the opposition is an obstacle to development. He wants to run the government unchallenged, un-criticised, and unopposed. Unlawfully and unconstitutionally banning political rallies and demonstrations, Magufuli has been saying that his regime has no space for opposition.

A week earlier, he had banned live broadcast of parliamentary proceedings on January 27, 2016, denying citizens the most popular TV programme they had enjoyed for 10 years consecutively. Initially, unaware of the negative impact the ban would eventually have on the the country's politics and on their party's future, members of the ruling party - which had been losing ground in major public debates - supported his move to deny the opposition and extra window through which they reached and impressed the people. Three years on, the ban is equally strangling the ruling party as it does to the opposition. The only politician left to do active politics and enjoy live coverage is Magufuli.

Opposition members of parliament who defied this order suffered ugly consequences. They encountered a series of life threats and harassments. Despite their parliamentary immunity, some of them were arrested and humiliated many times within the precincts of the parliament for statements made in connection with their responsibilities as members of parliament.

Others were arraigned in court for framed up charges. It was no wonder, therefore that the leader of official opposition, Freeman Mbowe, and MP for Tarime Urban, Esther Matiko, spent 104 days, including the 2018 Christmas season, in remand prison for reason associated with the judiciary's efforts to please the president in his efforts to suffocate the opposition. Mbowe and Matiku are part of 13 members of parliament in court for framed up charges associated with their defiance of Magufuli's order to ban political activities. Magufuli wants the opposition leaders locked out before 2020 elections for him to have a smooth ride.

Persecutions against Mbowe started in 2016 when Magufuli ordered the demolition of Club Bilicanas, one of Mbowe's main businesses and possibly Tanzania's most darling and earliest night club in the entertainment industry. The government confiscated his building and flattened it, and destroyed all furniture and music equipment in the club. *Tanzania Daima* newspaper - belonging to Mbowe family - that rented in the same building, was equally attacked, its equipment seized and destroyed.

A year later, a district commissioner in Hai District brutally demolished Mbowe's greenhouse by dismantling all material and disconnecting water pipes. Thereafter, Mafuguli promoted the district commissioner to regional commissioner and transferred him elsewhere. Mbowe's persecutions in his other businesses never ended, with intent to frustrate him by crippling his personal economy. It emanates from Magufuli's conviction that frustrating opposition leaders is the best strategy to paralyse masses behind them. Magufuli believes that an economically embattled Mbowe would not be able to strategise, organise, motivate, and lead a strong opposition.

A similar treatment was given to Lowassa, the opposition's former flag bearer. His son-in-law was charged with money laundering without bail since April 2016, and his several farms were confiscated, while a hefty tax was imposed on his businesses. Besides economic persecutions, Magufuli employed political tricks, using Rostam Aziz - one of Lowassa's longtime comrades - to "court" him with promises of releasing the son-in-law and offering him economic relief. When the state pressure became too unbearable and the promises looked too good to neglect, Lowassa suddenly quit the opposition and rejoined his old party in March 2019, probably putting a final nail in his political coffin.

Tanzanians have witnessed acts of political thuggery, prosecutions and casualties never seen before. It was during this period that one of the most critical members of parliament, Tundu Lissu, had a close shave from an attempted assassination as a gang of killers opened gunfire on him. The government's behaviour towards him before and after the shooting incident directly implicated it. Joseph Mbilinyi (an MP for Mbeya Urban) served a five-month sentence in jail for criticising President Magufuli and for linking him to the shooting of Lissu. On the same count and serving the sentence with Mbilinyi, was Emmanuel Masonga, his party's zonal secretary.

Incidents of maiming, abducting, drowning, shooting and killing political opponents increased to unprecedented proportions to cater for Magufuli's declaration of not tolerating any opposition. In fact, the horrible incidents started within weeks of his presidency when, on November 15, 2015, a group of zealots from Magufuli's party in his home region, Geita, attacked and lynched **ALPHONCE MAWAZO,** a charismatic regional chairman for the main opposition party. The horrible episode occured in broad daylight at about 12:30. He breathed his last about four hours later. Todate, no one has been held responsible.

That was the first case in a long list of horrible events against opposition politicians, activists, journalists, artists and others criticising Magufuli's leadership. The following is a random list of sample cases that exemplify Magufuli's brutality against opposing or dissenting voices:

BEN SAANANE – An assistant to CHADEMA national chairman and Leader of Official Opposition in Parliament: He was abducted in November 2016, weeks after he had been threatened for posting on his Facebook page, his doubts on the authenticity of President Magufuli's PhD credentials. The government has ignored public outcries and demands for police investigation into the matter. He is still missing. Some sources say he was severely tortured for one year and killed in late 2017.

DANIEL JOHN – CHADEMA ward secretary at Hananasifu, Dar es Salaam: In the evening of 12th February 2018, he was abducted, murdered and dumped at Coco Beach in Dar es Salaam. His co-abductee, Reginald Malya, had a narrow shave with severe machete slashes on his body.

AQUILINA AQUILINE – A university student: She was shot dead as police used live bullets to disperse opposition supporters after a CHADEMA campaign rally at Kinondoni Mkwajuni, Dar es Salaam, on 16th February 2018. Several others, including Isack Ng'aga, Erick John, and Aida Ulomi, were injured with bullets.

GODFREY LUENA – CHADEMA councilor in Namawala, Morogoro: He was slashed to pieces with machetes and axes by ruling party zealots at his home on 22nd February 2018.

AZORY GWANDA – A reporter with *Mwananchi* newspaper: He was abducted on 21st November 2017 as he was doing investigation on "a string of murders of officials and police" in Kibiti district. About 300 residents of Kibiti and Mkuranga were abducted and killed in a silent operation involving police and other state organs. In retaliation, some citizens killed police suspected officers. Tens of bodies were seen floating in the Indian ocean between 2016 and 2017, most of them washed away on unidentified. The Magufuli government took no action to arrest the killers until they were done with their mission. In may 2018, a member of parliamentarian for Kigoma Urban, Zitto Kabwe, presented to parliament a list of 68 names of some of the missing people. He demanded government action to no avail. Azory Gwanda was abducted in the middle of his investigation of these killings. Since 21st November 2017, he is still missing. Gwanda is now listed among the top 10 press freedom cases in the world.

TUNDU LISSU - The opposition chief whip, then President of the Tanganyika Law Society (TLS), and

MP for Singida East: He was gunshot on 7th September 2017 at his residence in Dodoma, shortly after he had attended a morning parliamentary session. He survived miraculously, was rushed to Nairobi Hospital in Kenya where he received treatment for four months until January 2018. He was later flown to Brussels for further treatment. The government has been reluctant to investigate the matter.

ROMA MKATOLIKI – Hip-hop singer Ibrahim Mussa a.k.a Roma Mkatoliki and three colleagues (famous for lyrics that sound critical to the establishment): Roma, Moni Central Zone, Charles (Bin Laden), and Emmanuel were kidnapped and tortured by armed people on 5th April 2017 at Tongwe Record Studio, Dar es Salaam. They were released after three days. When Roma called reporters, the information minister sat by his side at a press conference to censor his speech.

SALUM MOHAMED ALMASI – A student at University of Dar es Salaam Computing Centre (UCC). He was also an imam at Al- Kheri Mosque, Kurasini. Police shot him dead on 14th May 2017.

ALI JUMA SULEIMAN – An information director for Magharibi A District A, Zanzibar: He was kidnapped, tortured by secret police on 28th September 2017. He passed away while on treatment at hospital the following day.

SILVESTER MIGA – councilor for Kimwani, Muleba: He was attacked and lynched by "unknown people" at his home on the evening of 1st February 2016.

NAPE NNAUYE: - Former Minister of Information: He was threatened in public by a man with a pistol near

Protea Hotel, Dar es Salaam, on 23rd March 2017 as plain cloth police attempted to stop him from addressing a press conference after he was relieved of his ministerial duties. It was later found out that the man was a intelligence agent working with the presidential security unit.

SALMA SAID: – Reporter with Mwananchi newspaper: In March 2016, unknown assailants abducted and beat up Salma Said as she was preparing to report on the Zanzibar repeat election that was boycotted by the opposition. Also working as correspondent for *Deutsche Welle*, Salma was released by assailants after the election.

MAXENCE MELLO – A founder of *JamiiForums*, defender and champion of freedom of expression, digital security and freedom of information: On 13th December 2016, police apprehended and detained Maxence Melo. Three days later, he was arraigned on charges of refusing to reveal to police names of anonymous contributors to his blog.

YERIKO NYERERE and BOLLENT NGETTI: In June 2017, the two people were arraigned on charges of publishing "seditious statements" on their Facebook pages. Nyerere is a businessman; Ngetti is a journalist with *Sauti Huru* weekly newspaper. Over 50 social media users were arrested in 2017 alone for criticizing the president.

HALIMA MDEE - National chairperson for CHADEMA women's wing (BAWACHA)**:** In July 2017 police arrested and detained her for more than a week for criticizing

President Magufuli's stance on denying teen mothers a second chance to education.

ALI MASOUD – A Cartoonist: On January 1st 2018 police arrested Ali Masoud aka Masoud Kipanya on the grounds that his critical caricature were insulting the president.

SOCIAL MEDIA ACTIVISTS: Tens of social media users have been taken to court on charges of "sedition and insulting the president. In 2018, at least two cybercrime suspects were convicted. Bob Wangwe, was sentenced to eighteen months imprisonment or a fine of five million shillings ($2,500). Issack Habakuki was sentenced to three years in prison or a fine of seven million shillings ($3,500). Both of them paid the fine.

CHACHA HECHE SUGUTA: Younger brother to Tarime Rural MP, John Heche. He died under police custody at Sirari Police station on 27th April 2018. He was stabbed with a knife in his back, while handcuffed from behind. He died instantly. No one was held responsible.

MDUDE NYAGALI - a computer software trader an technician, social media activist and critic of President Magufuli. He was arrested, tortured, prosecuted several times between August 2016 and May 2019. Twice - on April 18, 2017 and May 24, 2018 - Mdude defeated the government in court, then instituted charges against government officials, seeking legal redress. On the evening of May 4, 2019 masked and armed police officers hijacked him at his office in Vwawa township, within 200 metres of Regional Police Headquarters in Songwe. Police denied involvement or knowledge of the incident, and initially refused to have it officially recorded. Eye witnesses said the incident involved four hijackers in two cars. In the course of forcefully dragging him from his shop to one of their vehicles, the men severely beat him up as he resisted and shouted for help. After a public outcry through social media and pressures from various fronts, the hijackers dumped Mdude in a bush, probably hoping he would be dead.

On the 5th day, a few days after three lawyers had filed a criminal application suing police and security authorities over the abduction and unlawful detention of Mdude, villagers found him abandoned in Makwenje village, Inyala ward, in Mbeya region. They raised alarm and people rushed to the place for his rescue.

SIMON KANGUYE: Chairman for Kakonko District Council in Kigoma region. On July 20, 2017, one day before President Magufuli's tour of Kibondo District, Kanguye was taken from his office for interrogation with the District Security Officer. The interrogation took place in the District Executive Director's office within the same premises. He has been missing since then. Two years on, Kanguye's whereabouts remain unknown.

I AM A SURVIVOR of an abduction incident from chih I escaped with the skin of my teeth in early October 2017. The assailants had been assigned to abduct and assassinate me for consistently criticising the president through a weekly column, *Maswali Magumu (Tough Questions)* in *MwanaHALISI* newspaper. Good Samaritans, including local and international human rights organizations, whisked me away and kept me in hiding for months within and beyond Tanzania. This is the first ever known scenario to me of a Tanzanian journalist surviving an attempted abduction and seeking political asylum in Europe.

The list of victims goes on and on, involving others shot and killed under police custody at police stations. In late December 2018, Magufuli said police who would shoot and kill "criminals" by accident should not be prosecuted but, on the contrary, they should be promoted and awarded. In short, Magufuli has criminalised opposition politics, using police and the army to militarise the country's elections. As a result, in 2018, the opposition unanimously decided to abstain from by-elections scheduled before 2020 which, besides being brutally militarised, cost the government billions of shillings unnecessarily. In three constituencies alone, the government spent 12 billion shillings on violent, sham by-elections whose winners had been predetermined by the state.

At different intervals, some opposition members of parliaments and councillors were terrorised and corrupted with financial or political gifts, in effort to make them cross over to the ruling party, as they were instructed to castigate the opposition and praise Magufuli for the "wonderful work" he has been doing. Some of them were immediately awarded with senior government posts.

With intent to technically control and suffocate the opposition, Magufuli has influenced the parliament to amend the Political Parties Act. The new law muzzles the parties' freedom and people's rights to exercise politics. With this law, Magufuli is putting all parties under his armpit by using the registrar of political parties. The registrar, an appointee of the president, will determine who should be member or leader of any political party.

Strong candidates likely to fiercely challenge Magufuli in 2020 elections are on the verge of being struck out of their parties' membership. Strong personalities likely to lead the opposition into a formidable force would be easily barred from vying for leadership positions in their own parties. It remains the registrar's discretion to determine the fate of any political party. The registrar of political parties has been granted powers to deregister any party without consulting any authorities., and he has been granted immunity against prosecution.

When the High Court of Tanzania, on 10th May 2019, nullified provisions 7 and 7A of the National Elections Act that gave highly politicised district executive directors powers to act as returning officers during elections, it was literally frustrating Magufuli who appointed them and instructed them to make sure his party wins by hooks or crooks. In one of his reckless public statements, Magufuli was quoted saying he would not tolerate any returning officer who would "give victory" to an opposition candidate. Showing outright fear of the opposition, Magufuli is on record telling them, on one official occasion: "How can you declare an opposition candidate as a winner when it is me who takes care of you, provides you with cars, and pays your salaries?"

Most, if not all, of executive district directors are staunch members or cadres of his party - against constitutional requirements and values of professionalism and impartiality. In fact, most of them have previously contested and lost parliamentary elections on the ruling party's ticket.

With all this, Magufuli feels suffocated by the opposition, and he is attempting to give himself a breathing space as he works out a strategy to take Tanzania back to a one-party rule through a back door. It remains to be seen if the people of Tanzania will give in to his shrewd initiatives meant to obliterate democratic gains experienced since 1992. By all standards, this is the highest expression of his cowardice.

The negative consequences of Magufuli's fear of opposition are enormous. Speaking during one parliamentary session in 2019, Kigoma Urban MP Zitto Kabwe, an economist by profession, said the oppression had not enabled Magufuli to raise the standard of living of his people. For instance, he said, between 2007 and 2012 when the democratic space was expanding in Tanzania under Jakaya Kikwete, one million people were liberated from the poverty line. The trend has been adversely reversed in the first three years of Magufuli's regime, he said, quoting IMF reports, according to which two million people had fallen into poverty under Magufuli between 2015 and 2018.

It is obvious that fear of the opposition makes Magufuli strategise ways to control civic movements and opinion, freedom of expression, and all democratic practices in various ways. And by so doing, he has negatively impacted on Tanzania's economic development. Moreover, he is putting his nation in political jeopardy because when people are denied a breathing space, they will find a way of expressing their opinions or actions, even if it means going against the law. This fact explains why under one-party rule between 1965 and 1992, Tanzania survived eight attempted coups; while there has been no such attempts since 1992 when the country opened doors for democratic practice. Magufuli's fear of opposition is detrimental to him and to his nation.

HIS FEAR OF RELIGIOUS LEADERS

In one instance, he confessed to his aides that the bishops' pastoral letters had destabilised him so much that he was determined to show them he was 'the only president in the country.'

In November 2001 some religious leaders predicted that Tanzania would be under a dictatorship in a near future. At that time no one took them seriously. But the story was covered by some newspapers. *Mwananchi* newspaper ran the story: "*Viongozi wa dini, wanaharakati, wahofia rais ajaye atakuwa dikteta.*" It literally meant that religious leaders and activists worried about President Kikwete being succeeded by a dictator. Of course, they never anticipated it was going to be Magufuli. But once he was in power and his dictatorial prowess began to unfold, memories of their prediction lingered.

Magufuli would be rightly called a religious rebel. Born and raised a Catholic, he went to seminary aspiring to become a priest. A teenager then, in his second year at Katoke Junior Seminary, he committed two offences, one of them sadistic, that may have led to his expulsion. Following a brief quarrel with his classmate in a dormitory,

Magufuli picked a sharp razor blade and mercilessly cut his colleague. The victim was left bleeding from cuts all over his body. Protecting him from being expelled, fellow students never reported the incident to authorities. But his sadism was registered.

In the second offence, he put his classmates in trouble when he stole a Chemistry book from one of them, hid it and quietly pretended nothing had happened. In search of the thief, authorities tormented innocent students as he kept quiet. Then suspicion fell on him, and he was summarily dismissed. School authorities never gave him a second chance, and Magufuli went to join a private school in Mwanza, Lake Secondary School, where he sat for his national secondary school exams.

Since then, he developed a personal hatred against the Catholic Church. He later ditched the Catholic Church and joined fundamentalist Christian churches. His wife Janet also defected with him. They both became active members of a Nigerian televangelist TB Joshua and his Synagogue Church Of All Nations. This background perhaps explains why, as a leader, he is never keen on the matter of natural justice. To him, a mere suspicion of wrongdoing is enough ground for firing someone from office or haphazardly terminating a contract.

As a member of parliament and minister, Magufuli built a church off his pocket and donated it to "all christian churches" in Chato, his home constituency. The Roman Catholic Church and official Protestants declined to use it for theological reasons. Pentecostal churches used it. This added yet another reason for him to openly dislike some big churches. Through his connection with fundamentalist churches, he met Rev. Dr. Modest Kipilimba, whom he later came to appoint Director General of the Tanzania Intelligence and Security Services (TISS) after Kipilimba's brief stint with the National Electoral Commission during an election that made Magufuli president. Kipilimba doubles as pastor and chief of intelligence. Coincidentally, they share this bitterness against some churches.

During his presidential campaigns, the main churches held a cautious position on supporting him due sensitive information shared to them from senior intelligence people and ruling party cadres at the time. Worried about his supposedly mental health, the main churches were not optimistic about his presidential bid. They never vetted for him. Todate, some well informed people within the ruling party still blame the party elders and his predecessor, Jakaya Kikwete, for handpicking Magufuli and forcing intelligence forces to influence his victory through the National Electoral Commision.

Ruling party insiders confirm that he lost the 2015 presidential election but was declared winner to please Kikwete who had vowed to never let Edward Lowassa become president after him following a deeply rooted hatred emanating from internal politics that had led to scandals and necessitated Lowassa's resignation as prime minister in 2008.

Even when Lowassa obviously became the most popular presidential aspirant within CCM, Kikwete used his presidential discretion to remove Lowassa's name from the list of contestants without any explanation. Aggrieved and determined to become the next president,

Lowassa crossed over to the opposition and became its enigmatic and phenomenal flag bearer. But the electoral commission worked under strict instructions from President Kikwete to declare Magufuli the winner.

Even from his own party, there were no celebrations as is normally the case. Almost everyone was dumbfounded, confused and angry. But that was it. According to the constitution, once a presidential winner has been announced, it is over. No challenge, no appeal whatsoever is constitutionally or legally allowable. That is how easy it is for the ruling party to "constitutionally rig" a presidential election in Tanzania.

So, when Magufuli became president, the Roman Catholic made proactive efforts to restore him and his wife to the sacramental life. Earlier on, his wife had refused to participate in his campaign. One of his close family members was quoted as telling some confidants: "You want to vote for him because you do not know him. If he wins, people will regret." Like his wife, this member, also a female, knew it, and she hated being involved in a situation where people would have to "plough with their teeth." But no one heeded her word. The ruling party's determination to retain power overcame all other national interests.

In February and April 2018, the Tanzania Episcopal Conference (TEC) and Evangelical Lutheran Church in Tanzania (ELCT) separately issued strongly-worded pastoral letters reprimanding the government's blatant violation of human rights and the president's anti-democracy inclination disguised in his "anti corruption" move.

In retaliation, Magufuli threatened to deregister the churches. He personally instructed the registrar of societies to write letters of warning to the two biggest churches in Tanzania. Public opinion was negative towards his decision. The home affairs minister appeared sympathetic with the churches and went by public feelings. Magufuli fired him unceremoniously.

Since then, Magufuli has been declining, sometimes acquiescing, invitations to attend some functions of the two churches or meeting certain strong bishops. Several bishops have been questioned by police or immigration department on their citizenship status. Former TEC secretary general and some bishops' passports were confiscated in 2018. When one bishop's passport was given back to him secretly in 2019, the president personally instructed him to "shut his mouth." Some critical bishops have apparently been placed on a blacklist, secretly targeted by Magufuli's deadly "watu wasiojulikana" (the unknown people, a life-threatening gang that abducts people and kills them in cold blood).

Obviously, Magufuli's fears strong and influential religious leaders due to his dark past and current evils committed by his regime. He is not ready to answer their questions on the whereabouts of missing people. He is not ready to answer their questions on his blatant violation of the constitution. In one instance, he confessed to his aides that the bishops' pastoral letters had destabilised him so much that he was determined to show them he was "the only president in the country."

Gripped with fear, some church leaders are slowly giving in to his threats, in silent acquiescence granting him some of his wishes, and frequenting state house for recognition, photo opportunity and presidential endorsement. He is accused of attempting to censor their homilies and tampering with some of their public addresses before they are read out. At a celebration to mark 150 years of Catholicism in Tanzania held at Bagamoyo in November 2018, he created a silent division among bishops when some of them learnt of the state house's request to see in advance the speech by the President of the Tanzania Episcopal Conference. Sections of staunch Catholic believers complain silently about church leaders entertaining Magufuli's political gestures during their spiritual services by disrupting liturgical observances with his heavily loaded bodyguards and a crew of media personnel that seem to care less about spiritual devotion than about their boss, who takes advantage of a his presence at mass to gain political capital.

With an exception of a few Catholic bishops, and one senior Lutheran bishop in Dar es Salaam, Magufuli does not have a sincerely warm relationship with a collegiate of religious leaders from established churches. Apparently, his aides have been struggling to advise him on the essence of creating a good rapport with religious leaders. Once in late 2018 he invited TEC's leadership to state house and paradded them for a photo opportunity and generous comments on his leadership. Attempting to show a change of heart, he has been extending an offer to provide state security to some bishops as a way of enticing and weakening them.

A senior Catholic bishop recently declined that offer, and the state house has warned him that they would not be responsible in the event of him getting involved in an unexpected accident. But this bishop knew that his predecessor, who had been enjoying such state security and some favours, had unfortunately ended up compromising on certain matters of principle involving the state or the ruling party.

HIS FEAR OF MUSLIMS

Muslims already understand that he fears and dislikes them, and they hate the fact that he meets them when he thinks such an encounter would earn him some political mileage.

When Magufuli told Muslims, on 20th May 2019, that the government of Saudi Arabia had agreed to build a new Muslim university in Tanzania, insiders knew he was battling with his conscience about Muslims, standing with a sect of them to seek their support in style. But Magufuli is known to have a chronic distaste for Muslims. Some sources say he is also naive about Islam. When he came to power, he made two dangerous moves towards Muslims.

Firstly, he made a public promise to help BAKWATA - the Muslim Council of Tanzania, opposed and viewed by many Muslims as an organ of, and sympathetic to, the government - to recover its lost and stolen properties. He later claimed to have found out that most of the lost properties had been duly sold by former corrupt officials. He has not succeeded to honour his promise. Interestingly, there are more Muslims outside BAKWATA.

Therefore Magufuli's promises stirred up and revived internal rivalries between BAKWATA and their internal adversaries.

In another move, his right hand man, demagogic Paul Makonda, started collecting money from businesses and overseas cronies in order build BAKWATA headquarters. This confirmed the Muslim's long held beliefs.

Secondly, came Magufuli's move for tax exemption. He ordered an audit to establish abuses of tax exemptions. BAKWATA was eventually ordered to pay a lot of money for cars that never existed or which were already sold. Seemingly at war with Muslims, he is working hard to make sure they do not become united. He fears that a united Muslim community would become a formidable force when facing their historically common enemy - the government.

In Zanzibar, a predominantly Muslim state, Magufuli has lost grip due to the 2015 rigged elections. He offended them most when during one his tours to the isles he mobilized his party to discriminate against opposition members. There is also an issue of sheikhs from Zanzibar in remand prison without bail or trial. He associates their religion with terrorism. He fears that if they are released, they will mobilize fellow Muslims to unite and fight for their rights. It was later known that even when government forces killed hundreds of citizens in Kibiti district in a special operation that has left many questions unanswered, the hidden motive behind was to annihilate elements of terrorism and religious fundamentalism.

When he was approached by eminent people asking him to organise a national forum that would work on establishing peace and cordial understanding between his government and several groups, he cautiously agreed, but told them never to bring some Muslim groups, including BAKWATA, back into the forum. Muslims already understand that he fears and dislikes them, and they hate the fact that he meets them when he thinks such an encounter would earn him some political mileage.

HIS FEAR OF ZANZIBAR AND THE UNION

Even when police hijacked and forced the Zanzibar Electoral Commission chairman to nullify the results, suddenly and unconstitutionally, it only affected the Zanzibar presidential election results. Magufuli's votes remained unchanged. Even todate, he remains rejected in Zanzibar.

The union between Tanganyika and Zanzibar (to beget Tanzania) has been a political thorn in the flesh of all government phases since its inception in 1964. Julius Kambarage Nyerere, Tanzania's founding president, once said that had he been able, he would have "pushed the troublesome islands deep into the Indian ocean."

This union is one single factor that creates political uncertainty to every sitting president irrespective of the situation in both sides. It has caused deaths, detentions, assassinations, resignations, terminations, censorships, and successive vote rigging since 1995. As through it, Tanzania's sovereignty is gauged, then it can be safely said that on this single issue, Tanzania has been rising and falling since 1964.

With the ushering in of multiparty politics in 1992, Tanzania's political landscape as per union perspective changed dramatically. With successive vote rigging in Zanzibar, the union bred more critics and enemies than it did before 1992. All incoming new presidents have been vowing to maintain and protect the union. Because of its historical nature, the union requires more negotiations and diplomacy. Unfortunately, however, these leaders fear to open up for union discussion due to its shaky legal foundation.

Fear has a cross-cutting phenomenon among government leaders. So, Magufuli is not spared of the fear for union. This fear leads him to sidelining Zanzibar in many of his political and administrative decisions.

In Mwalimu Nyerere's pivotal speech of 1995, as he spoke about the challenges the country was facing, he mentioned the union as one of major cracks in the nation. Despite his eloquence and steady confidence, Mwalimu Nyerere was shaken by union matters. He feared a lot about it, and so did his successors.

Repeatedly in his private discussions, former president Mkapa has been mentioning the Zanzibar bloody crash with the opposition in January 2001 as one of his regime's blind spots. His impunity in justifying the vote rigging, killed tens of people and produced refugees. Todate, he is still haunted by this awful event.

Mkapa's immediate successor, Jakaya Kikwete, may be hailed to being able to stabilise the union for some time. Through his diplomatic leadership and his close relationship with his Zanzibar counterpart, Amani Karume, an amicable relation had been reached between warring factions in Zanzibar. As one of the results of their initiative, an independent election committee comprising equal members from two main parties was formed. When he formed the constitutional review committee close to the end of his presidency, Kikwete gave the people a breathing space as they proposed a form of union they prefered. But he messed up at the eleventh hour when, through the influence of some elders, he overturned people's views on the new constitution, mainly for fear of Zanzibar being autonomous.

Magufuli does not have enough political acumen to deal with union matters. Nor does he possess enough humility to allow his deputies to deal with it on his behalf. His unexpected rise into power, came through the most visible vote rigging process since 1995. Zanzibar opposition flag bearer Maalim Seif Sharif Hamad evidently won the Zanzibar election with 207,847 votes (52.8 percent) against Mohamed Shein's 182,011 votes (46.2 percent). As union presidential candidate, Magufuli garnered the least votes from Zanzibar - 194,317 (46.5 percent) against Edward Lowassa's 211,033 (50.5 percent).

Even when police hijacked and forced the Zanzibar Electoral Commission chairman to nullify the results, suddenly and unconstitutionally, it only affected the Zanzibar presidential election results. Magufuli's votes remained unchanged. Even todate, he remains rejected in Zanzibar. Despite calls by local and international bodies for the union leadership to address the Zanzibar situation "for the sake of democracy and the country," the authorities (first Kikwete, then Magufuli) never seemed to be bold enough to take action. Guilt was eating them up.

In CCM's narrow point of view, Hamad's victory was putting the union on the verge of breaking up. Of course, it was going to effect changes in the structure of the union - which they did not want to happen. As a result, they used the army and police to influence the electoral commission chairman, and Zanzibar went back into a crisis it was about to overcome.

While every person in their right senses knew all this, in the midst of a crisis as everyone questioned the legitimacy of a sham runoff election scheduled for March 2016, and with Magufuli already installed as the union president, the optimistic media wanted to get his position and reaction, and whether he would intervene to stop this outright political thuggery. He disappointed everyone when he said his hand were tied, claiming he had no constitutional mandate to intervene in the Zanzibar election impasse. Yet when the sham election was re-organised in March, when he faced the prospects of the opposition holding demonstrations to protest the re-run of the elections, Magufuli sent his troops to terrorise voters in Zanzibar.

Using the army against his own citizens, - over whom he had claimed to have no powers - he intimidated the opposition, reminding them that he was commander-in-chief of the armed forces ready take a stern action against any demonstrators. The sham runoff election was shunned by the opposition. CCM's Dr. Shein was declared winner with 91.4 percent after competing against his own shadow. That was Magufuli's first expression of his fear of Zanzibar and the union.

Clearly, the 2015 election in Zanzibar, broke up the then government of unity that had brought together CCM and CUF in one cabinet. This historical formulation had been a result of negotiations between President Amani Karume and Maalim Seif Sharif Hamad. It had created a peaceful political environment that has been wiped out by Magufuli's bullish style of leadership.

His fear of the union hangs on a couple of factors, namely, his inability to negotiate with Zanzibaris and, secondly, his fear of unearthing his own vote rigging. His sincere plea is not to touch it until he goes out of state house.

There is yet one more fear factor. Since President Ali Hassan Mwinyi (1985-95), there has never been a union president from Zanzibar. Although it is not a constitutional matter, political logic would put it for one to think that under this political volatility, wisdom should lead the leadership to accommodate this factor. It has not happened, and its consequences cannot be underestimated politically.

Zanzibaris, irrespective of their parties, grumble about Zanzibar being swallowed by Tanganyika. When Magufuli cannot negotiate or rectify union anomalies, it then justifies iron-fist approach to union matters.

Lack of wisdom and sensitivity slapped former Vice President Mohammed Ghalib Bilal. As vice president under Kikwete, he was one of potential presidential contenders. One would have thought that protocol sensitivity would have been applied to promote him at least to the five finalists. He did not, and no one came out to explain this.

For a junior minister like January Makamba to sail above a sitting vice president within a party that is not governed democratically, is not only an embarrassment but a clear initiative to sideline Zanzibar. Gharib Bilal has since disappeared from political limelight.

HIS FEAR OF ORGANISED WORKERS

Clearly, Magufuli has antagonised himself with workers for his careless handling of their concerns. Tanzania has about 300,000 civil servants and a bit over 2 million private sector employees. But their social influence is wider than their numbers. No sensible politician would ignore their impact, but Magufuli has been forcing them to "work with their teeth."

At the state house in Dar es Salaam on December 28, 2018, Magufuli met top executives for the Public Service Social Security Fund (PSSSF), National Social Security Fund (NSSF), and Social Security Regulatory Authority (SSRA) and overturned his government's controversial formula on calculating retirement benefits, giving in to pressure from pensioners, workers, and the opposition.

Under the new controversial formula, pensioners would receive 25 percent in lump-sum payment of their benefits, spreading the remaining 75 percent in monthly payments for 13 years. Obviously, Magufuli's sudden change of heart was meant to win political capital against his own government's position that was being pushed in parliament, twice prompting critical press conferences from the responsible shadow minister Esther Bulaya. A week earlier, the Member of Parliament for Kibamba, John Mnyika, had requested the president to reconsider the government's unfriendly position on the matter.

Seemingly critical of his ministers and officers, as if he had not been involved in its planning and signing it into a law that came into effect on 1st August 2018, Magufuli made this u-turn in the meeting that was broadcast live. The drafting of the regulations had been done in 2014 when he was a cabinet minister, and it was almost being passed during his third year as president. But the the noises became unbearable.

To people who know Magufuli's position on the matter, this was mere propaganda meant to catch attention of the workers and their sympathisers. For one thing, his first three years have shown how Magufuli has always been taking workers for granted. He seems to be oblivious of the fact that his immediate predecessor's negligent and unpalatable statement on workers' rights almost cost him the presidency in 2010. Coupled with corruption concerns affecting the government then, Jakaya Kikwete's mishandling of workers had him struggle to woo voters. It was unfortunate that Magufuli never learnt a lesson from what had befallen Kikwete.

On May Day 2018, Magufuli blatantly told workers that he had no intention of considering their pay rise because he was focused on constructing the standard gauge railway. Interestingly, the railway did not have anything to do with workers' pay because it is funded by a foreign loan. Workers' salaries are paid with internal collections. For three years, Magufuli has literally refused to grant the workers' annual salary increment - which is statutory; and he has put a halt on their statutory promotions. Besides, he has fired thousands of workers in the pretext of cleaning up the system from ghost workers and holders of fake certificates.

While he should have been credited for taking such stern actions, he was forced to pay the price of his double standards. Some of his close associates, including his beloved crony and regional commissioner for Dar es Salaam Paul Makonda fall, in the same - even worse - category, but he spared and praised them in public for doing a great job "despite their illiteracy."

Sometimes, he got himself in trouble for making contradictory statements. While he was boasting of his government having "enough money" to accomplish great development projects, he, at the same time, told workers to bear with him because the government "has no money."

Clearly, Magufuli has antagonised himself with workers for his careless handling of their concerns. Tanzania has about 300,000 civil servants and a bit over 2 million private sector employees. But their social influence is wider than their numbers. No sensible politician would ignore their impact, but Magufuli has been forcing them to "work with their teeth."

Little did he expect the workers' teeth to bite into his flesh. And while he was busy considering a rebuff for pensioners, as he enjoyed his surrogates' temporary cheers on the evening of December 28, 2018, the workers' demands were still not taken care of. He was still terrorised by the same people he was attempting to terrorise. With three years of the workers' misery, the fear he was struggling to instill in them is finding its way back into himself.

HIS FEAR OF PARLIAMENT

The president has weakened the national assembly speaker, consequently paralysing the parliament, because as a former parliamentarian, he knows what vibrant parliaments can do to corrupt and irresponsible governments.

On 7th January 2019, the Speaker of the National Assembly, Job Ndugai, held a press conference and, through media, ordered the Controller and Auditor General (CAG), Prof. Mussa Assad, to appear before the parliamentary ethics committee, which would grill him on allegations of disrespecting the parliament in one of his comments when responding to a question by a foreign media. Prof. Assad had been quoted as saying Tanzania's parliament was weak for failing to take the government to task following evidence of corrupt practices availed to the parliament in CAG's annual reports. The CAG was responding to a reporter's question as to why his office was doing nothing after unveiling government corruption in its annual reports.

Prof. Assad said, in Kiswahili: "That is the task of the parliament. If we are producing reports, yet no action is being taken, to me, that is the weakness of the parliament... I believe it is a challenge that will be worked on... the parliament is failing is failing to exercise its powers effectively."

The speaker's response was unnecessarily bitter, accusing the CAG for speaking badly about his country while abroad. So, he ordered Prof. Assad to report to the parliamentary committee willingly, or else he would be forcefully taken "in handcuffs."

Of course, the constitution protects the CAG from such interferences and threats, but under Magufuli the constitution and laws do not matter. He has been trampling on everybody and every institution, claiming the executive is more powerful than other pillars. Without any doubt, he has succeeded in overpowering the speaker, making him subservient and obedient to the president and the executive. On several occasions he has ordered the speaker and his deputy to help him silence critical members of parliament, particularly the opposition.

And the speaker has been misusing parliamentary regulations to threaten critics and drag parliamentary debates in favour of the government regardless of national interests at stake. So, when the speaker came out with his outburst against the CAG, giving orders that cannot be guaranteed by laws or constitution, informed minds understood h was pushing a government's agenda to silence the parliament. In essence, the speaker was proving the weakness of his parliament.

The president has weakened the speaker, consequently paralysing the parliament, because as a former parliamentarian, he knows what vibrant parliaments can do to corrupt and irresponsible governments. That is why one of his first blows against democracy started with banning live coverage of parliamentary sessions in 2016. During his time as minister, major cabinet reshuffles under President Kikwete emanated from parliamentary debates. All major scandals involving senior government officials were unveiled by the parliament, picked by media.

No wonder the public knows less about government corruption under Magufuli, and some uninformed foreign media brand him as "a corruption bulldozer." In fact, he has become a "corruption incubator" because his tactic to ban live coverage of parliamentary debates since January 2016 and to silence members of parliament through the speaker, has mostly worked in his favour, denying people useful information.

His fear of parliament has forced him to instill fear into parliamentarians. The greatest threats of them all happened on 7th September 2017 when "unknown people" attempted to assassinate Tundu Lissu at his home shortly after addressing a morning parliamentary session.

For the entire period of the MP's agony and treatment in Kenya and Belgium, the president and the speaker remained openly hostile. Not even a get well soon message was sent, let alone parliamentary officers to check on him. The parliament, which is legally required to pay for his treatment, never issued a single cent - seeking to please the president. While so many private institutions and individuals made public statements against the horrendous shooting against the member of parliament, not a voice was heard from the speaker or his parliamentary staff.

Several draconian laws that have been bringing adverse effects in the country were passed, and are being passed, by the parliament under orders from the state house. When the CAG reports unveiled a loss of Tshs 1.5 trillion (later verified to be Tshs 2.4 trillion) in the 2016/2017 budget, the parliament did not take any serious action against the government. Only it took the president to invite the CAG and treasurer general Dotto James (who happens to be the president's nephew), and ask them during one of his regular presidential live broadcasts, "if the government had hidden the 1.5 trillion."

On several occasions, the speaker has been using police to forcefully take "troublesome" opposition members of parliament from parliamentary floor - even banning them from attending parliament for several months. - when he faces stiff criticism from them. Once, President Magufuli applauded the speaker for such a bold decision that would deny the MPs the immunity they employ in quizzing the government; and that while they are outside parliament, he (the president) would deal with them squarely if they dared to criticise him.

When MPs from Tanzania's Southern block became bitter against the government's move to confiscate billions of shillings from the Cashewnut Board of Tanzania in 2018, the speaker forced them to act in the government's interests. Weeks later, in one of his live addresses at the state house, President Magufuli's commended the speaker for the job well done, and warned the MPs who had threatened to organise huge public demonstrations in their constituencies.

Magufuli said he would literally "beat up their aunts," starting with the Prime Minister's own aunt. He was implingly accusing the Prime Minister, Kassim Majaliwa, of colluding with the bitter MPs because he also hails from the southern block. Threatening to beat up the MP's relatives was a clear indication of the president's fear of the parliament that he has been struggling to subdue completely.

So, when the Parliament finally announced on April 2, 2019 that it had resolved to "never work with CAG Assad," it was a culmination of Magufuli's plan to silence the parliament. Magufuli is blatantly anti-democracy, anti-audit, and excessively anti-transparency. With this decision from the parliament that is controlled by the majority from the ruling party, by fighting allies who should have been helping the government to fight corruption, one wonders how he can fight corruption without open and free media, free civil society, free opposition, free speech, free assembly, free parliament, free association, and now free audit.

HIS FEAR OF INTELLIGENCE AND SECURITY SERVICES

He had his best contacts mainly within the infrastructure industry, which he had led as minister for almost two decades. He cared less about other sectors, particularly the intelligence service which, for some reason, he had silently branded as "dangerous."

Like the late Idi Amin, Uganda's former dictator, Magufuli's number one policy is political survival. People close to him share a view that he has a high sense of insecurity. To some of his aides, Magufuli appear to be a controversial dichotomy between a Christian and a pagan. Much as as his sense of insecurity takes him to christian services - posing for photo opportunities with bishops, pastors and priests - it equally takes him to secret "unchristian" ceremonies, particularly in his hometown, Chato.

He will do anything that he hopes can keep him safe and secure at least for some time. But the bad thing is that, out of this sense of insecurity, he has resorted to a strategy that makes him keep instilling a sense of fear to his people. Disloyalty, criticism or opposition are mercilessly punished.

In a similar way that Amin recruited army men from certain tribes and removed others, brutally removing the Langi and Acholi from the armed forces, Magufuli has been recruiting many of his tribesmen for the intelligence service and army mostly without adhering to laid down procedures. This has led into him getting the wrong people into the system. Just as Amin recruited his tribesmen and Nubianas from Sudan into the Ugandan army as a way of assuring himself complete loyalty, Magufuli has been recruiting staff into sensitive positions, mainly from his Sukuma tribe or his home zone - Lake Victoria Zone.

Just as Idi Amin promoted Col. Isack Maliyamungu, his tribesman and relative, for his loyalty and obedience in carrying out vicious killings of his critics, Magufuli has, against all odds, promoted and endeared Paul Makonda as his most trusted henchman and untouchable right-hand man, in whose hands many people have suffered serious consequences of being on the wrong side of Magufuli.

Within the ranks of Magufuli's hit squad (the unknown people), Makonda is nicknamed "bosi mtoto," meaning the "little boss." Despite his obvious corrupt and demagogic lifestyle, Makonda is one of Magufuli's most trusted and protected "assistants" to whom the president even assigned special guards from his presidential security unit. He is probably one of his government's most corrupt officials.

Magufuli came to power with a baggage of ignorance about the intelligence system of Tanzania. Surprisingly, he was one of few ministers who served in various ministries without being vetted. Unlike his predecessors, Magufuli found himself in a security network of which he knew little concerning its operations, ethics and technicalities. He had his best contacts mainly within the infrastructure industry, which he had led as minister for almost two decades. He cared less about other sectors, particularly the intelligence service which, for some reason, he had silently branded as "dangerous."

Some of those who have worked closely to him say Magufuli has a character that seeks to link service more with personalities than with professionalism, principle or competence. So, when he assumed power, because of fear and distrust to the people that surrounded him, he branded most senior officers as "belonging" to their previous bosses - who he did not trust; and he accused some of them of having colluded with the opposition during the 2015 general election, which he won with much ado. He came to office bent on cleaning up the security service. He made many unprofessional and unvetted appointments into the system, some of whom have eventually become a thorn in the flesh of his very system.

Within the ruling party ranks, he had never assumed any leadership; never had been part of the Central Committee, hence creating a vacuum of skills and knowledge on how to deal with a complex security system. With such ignorance, there were two dangerous routes he could take - and he did.

One was to hastly order operations without demanding the analysis of collateral damage. Blindly, he ordered several actions that backfired afterwards and caused mischiefs. For instance, he haphazardly fired several regional security officers on the ground that they had sabotaged him during his presidential campaign. He accused them of having given him false briefing regarding his popularity, and that they had wrongly projected his victory. The truth is, some of them had allegedly given him wrong information because he had insisted, in their presence, to get positive information; and they had not been professional enough to let him swallow a bitter pill. So, even as a candidate he was already behaving as boss, terrorising junior security officers; and out of fear, they deceived him.

Fearing insiders and experienced staff, he opted to appoint as director general someone who principally was deemed not competent enough for the top post of the intelligence system, but was seemingly loyal enough to him by religiously following the president's orders. This is how Dr. Modest Kipilimba, his former college mate at Mkwawa Teachers' College, suddenly rose to the highest ranks within TISS. To many observers within the security service, based on his shady career history, Dr. Kipilimba was not the system's natural choice.

A former secondary school teacher who had had a stint at the Bank of Tanzania and the National Identification Authority (NIDA), Kipilimba had served for 90 days as head of IT with the National Electoral Commission of Tanzania during the 2015 elections. Magufuli believed Kipilimba had been personally involved in rigging presidential votes in his favour; although insiders within the ruling party say that even with Kipilimba's original efforts, their candidate never went beyond 49 percent of the total votes after two rigging attempts. Extra "tactics" were needed to raise the figures to 58 percent, particularly after police had been involved in confiscating tallying equipment of the opposition, temporarily incarcerating the tallying officers.

Even the TISS boss felt insecure and lacked confidence in the presence of experienced, properly trained, and more qualified senior staff. To cover up for his weak profile, and to assert his authority, the new TISS boss resorted to giving total obedience to the president. In addition, he carried out massive appointments of new security operatives.

Many of these operatives were given short training lasting between one month and one year and, against established procedures, they were subsequently put in charge of sensitive departments. Some of them were assigned to work in various government parastatals such as Tanzania Revenue Authority (TRA), Tanzania Ports Authority (TPA), Prevention and Combating of Corruption Bureau (PCCB), Tanzania Telecommunications Company Limited (TTCL), Bank of Tanzania (BoT), foreign ministry and other sensitive offices.

Unfortunately, some of these security officers, apart from lacking professional training, have had criminal records prior to their appointment, and they still conducted themselves corruptly. For instance, one Isack Bwire, is on record for being injured by gunshots in a criminal incident involving security operatives and a businessman in Mara region in 2018. Another one, Edward Moses, was fired from the PCCB for serious misconduct in early 2019. These two men were among intelligence officers who had been hurriedly hired and put in incharge of sensitive matters, against professional etiquettes.

It all emanates from the president's ignorance of the intelligence system, and his quest for total obedience from the same people that should be advising him. In principle, the intelligence boss should be the president's chief advisor on sensitive matters of national interest. But with Magufuli, it is the other way round. He is the chief advisor to the intelligence boss; and security professionals are not happy about it, as it poses a great risk to the nation.

In early 2019, Magufuli fired a PCCB chief, Valentine Mlowola - his own appointment - following a their conversation between them in which Mlowola advised the president to take care of the strategic leadership and leave the operational, tactical part of PCCB to professionals. The president later replaced Mlowola with a police officer whom he (the president) had previously fired on grounds of dubious integrity. Following grumbles and advice on the way he had fired him, he reinstated him by appointing him to a junior post in a remote region, from where he picked him again to make him PCCB chief. Word is out that after this appointment, the TISS boss advised this new PCCB boss to "obey the president's commands as they come."

This approach of haphazardly hiring security operatives, though psychologically served to quell Magufuli and Kipilimba's insecurity, albeit temporarily, has caused much discomfort within the system, and it has become an unfortunate entry point for many rogue elements into the country's intelligence system. This is partly where the problem of "the unknown people" starts from.

There is another way of looking at it. As new president, Magufuli was easily overwhelmed by having access to sensitive information and secrets of some big personalities and institutions. With this amount of secrecy in his hands, he felt too powerful and he started misusing some information to blackmail some of his own security team members.

There is an outstanding fact that prior to 2015 elections Magufuli had been disqualified by the security team from running for president on health grounds. A recommendation was made to the central committee to disqualify him from running. But due to reasons beyond public eye, the report was never used during screening of presidential aspirants in his party. With a lot of pressure from the surging opposition alliance, Magufuli eventually emerged as a compromise choice, taking advantage of internal conflicts within the ruling party. The intelligence team that had disqualified him was forced to defend him and make sure that he wins.

With controversial election results out, the rift within the intelligence system was visible. Magufuli, through his ignorance of the system, started to make hasty decisions that exacerbated internal conflicts. That is how he started to immediately transfer some senior intelligence officers from state house to far reaching regions. He demoted most of them, and then he sweepingly made changes in all security organs.

The police force had a new chief after Magufuli accused the former IGP of insubordination. He replaced a veteran anti-corruption chief who was in hospital in Germany, and he appointed a first female to head the immigration department. On top of that, he appointed a new chief of intelligence mentioned above.

In the military, he appointed his tribe mate, Venance Mabeyo, from a lower rank and made him Chief of Defence Forces (CDF), causing chilling feelings within the military and thereby sending some senior generals outside the military jurisdiction. These changes created fear and insecurity within security organs, and this affected his future trust on them. Above all, he reached out to neighbouring Rwanda for assistance. Some sources point out that at one point, his security details were manned by Rwandese personnel, creating uncertainty around the presidency. As if that was not enough, a reserve security group was established to protect the president and to deal with threats, especially from the opposition.

That extra group was manned by the Dar es Salaam Regional Commissioner, Paul Makonda, who suddenly became so powerful and one of the most trusted cronies of the president. The Makonda group, purporting to protect the president from criticism, allegedly became highly responsible for tortures and extrajudicial killings famously attributed to "watu wasiojulikana" - the unknown people. With Magufuli relying on other security organs other than official TISS, a conflict was emerging where the public blamed official security advisors for not being responsible in curbing sinister actions of para security groups.

This led to numerous events. The president could no longer trust most of his official security personnel, including his personal doctor. His medical team was placed under a gynecologist who, in fact, had nothing to do with the president's health security. It was discovered later that the president had also hired an Israel-based doctor to attend to his medical needs. The disputed Chato airport has also to do with this external sourcing of security issues.

Besides, the public has been witnessing a narrowing security perimeter around the president. He is surrounded by highly visible machine guns. His motorcade is normally being monitored by at least two helicopters. Magufuli enjoys this security flamboyance, but his security team is heavily stressed by this display of dangerous arsenals around him. Essentially, it increases fear of the public and security personnel, and it facilitates possible fatal errors. Due to the dwindling trust among the presidential security team, there is little room to substituting security details. The same people are on his watch 24/7, and a danger of fatigue is apparent.

Magufuli is obsessed with the use of power. He has been parading heads of army and security organs in public events, sometimes asking them to give speech or contribute money at impromptu fundraising occasions. Some of the are annoyed but, instead of resisting, they grumble silently. Their traditional public impartiality has vanished, and now they are forced to sing and and dance to his endless tunes. Due to this obsession, he occasionally forces them to undertake certain missions recklessly. One infamous operation to which he is circumstantially linked is an assassination attempt of Tundu Lissu. He is said to have manned and micromanaged this operation - assisted by Makonda - and it ended ungracefully. Later on, as issues progressed, the president failed even to put on a hypocritical face to minimize the damage.

The "unknown people" also mismanaged the abduction of Mohamed Dewji - another event that also ended ungracefully. As a result, he decided to confiscate his plots of land in Tanga region. These two operations had little advice from the official security team under TISS - which he surprisingly accuses of corruption.

The infamous Mererani wall is another exhibit of Magufuli's mistrust of his security team. He embarked on this hasty decision with little advice from them. The national services chief and that of Tanzania People's Defence Force (TPDF) were the only ones responsible to him. As a results, the wall has not helped to stop the smuggling of *Tanzanite* as it was intended. Instead, it has partly caused economic shutdown. Furthermore, the wall has been used by external people (from a neighbouring country) to understand the vulnerability of our security system.

In fact, Magufuli has a deep mistrust of his own security team. He has destroyed career records of some well-trained security personnel. His mistrust of former TISS chiefs is without doubt a misguided approach and it undermines the security that protects him. He is on record confessing in public that he is hacking phones of his cabinet ministers. Besides being a criminal act, it shows without uncertainty that he does not trust his cabinet ministers. It also sends signals that even his security team phones connectivity can be hacked by his excellency.

But such mistrust by any president always creates self imprisonment. As a result of this, Magufuli is caged and selfcaged in the state house. His family members are also suffering from the same. In fact, he misses one cardinal principle that guides presidents and their security teams - having teams that advise them. On the contrary, he is renowned for being his advisors' advisor. And if there is any risk to the country's ultimate peace, security and stability, it is Magufuli's leadership style and his sense of insecurity.

HIS FEAR OF THE INTERNATIONAL COMMUNITY

> *"A strong voice that incessantly and successfully fought to liberate several African countries (from colonialism, dictatorship and Apartheid) is currently waning. A relentlessly tireless advocate for the global dignity of humanity has been recently missing out on a global diplomatic forum. What went wrong?"* - SAUTI KUBWA website

Magufuli's fear of the international community is explicit. In his first three years as president, he has exhibited his fear and hostility against the west, in what some observers note his obvious inferiority complex. To assert his power, however, he has opted to cheap propaganda by branding the west as imperialist when they question his commitment to democracy and human rights, but when he receives funds from them, he calls them "great men" or development partners,.

Between 2015 and 2018, six diplomats were kicked out of Tanzania for being on the wrong side of Magufuli. As a result, Tanzania's relations with many western countries and development partners were strained. Roeland van de Geer, then EU ambassador to Tanzania, was fired in November 2018, becoming the latest culprit then. Before him, five UN diplomats had been declared "unwanted" in Tanzania.

The list of rejected or expelled diplomats - within short notice - includes Anna Collins Falk, who was head of UN women in Tanzania; Awa Dabo, UNDP country manager; and Zulmira Mrita Rodrigues, UNESCO country manager.

The international community in Tanzania is represented by a community of diplomats, expatriates, foreign investors, international organizations and partnership networks with organisations based in Tanzania and overseas. This entity irritates Magufuli on several grounds and, thus, instills fear in him.

Magufuli fears the international community because of his reckless disregard to human rights. His understanding of human rights is questionable. He publicly argues that following codes of human rights would impede his vision and determination to develop his country. To him, human rights are anti-development. In his pursuit for the so called development, he unleashes attacks on human rights allies including the media, civil society organisations, and all champions of rule of law and open government system. To him, human rights are optional and can only be followed by countries that are already developed. He has insists, on many occasions, that human rights are tools of imperialism for stealing, plundering and under-developing the country.

To Magufuli, human rights activists are unpatriotic mercenaries of western imperialism.

Even when he chooses to consider human rights - for some reason - Magufuli thinks that every country is free to choose a set of human rights it should observe. This is where he asserts a rhetoric of sovereignty, saying he cannot be dictated by anybody from outside his country almost in a similar manner as Zimbabwe's Robert Mugabe did. From Magufuli's scanty knowledge of western countries, he bluffs that western countries are worse in terms of human rights violation. He categorically rejects the universality of human rights. As a result of this false understanding of human rights, Magufuli - being a chronic advisor of his advisors - lectures and forces his foreign affairs ministry to also either ignore international community or launch fruitless efforts to convince the world to accept his narrow view on human rights.

Obviously, Magufuli's fear of international community emanates from his lack of international exposure. He hardly travels abroad, claiming he is saving money. Of course, he and his cronies have been squandering billions of shillings within the country, according to audited reports by the controller and auditor general.

Magufuli has a communication deficiency when it comes to using international languages. His demeanour and dictatorial inclinations make him look screwed whenever advised to stick to written speeches. Interestingly, he has questionable reading skills. He embarrasses himself and his audience by making a lot of reading mistakes - sending him to short temperament, apt to leading him to breach of diplomatic etiquettes.

Driven by this fear of international community, Magufuli has frequently changed main officials of foreign affairs more than any of his predecessors. In a span of three years, he has changed three permanent secretaries for foreign affairs, two ministers, and two deputy ministers. He has fired one deputy minister. The list also includes ambassadors who were either fired or recalled. He appoints new ones after publicly scandalizing others. On top of that he is notorious for repatriating foreign diplomats. He accuses Tanzanian diplomats of failing to defend the country's interests, while claiming that foreign diplomats are interfering with internal matters of his country.

There is another reason for Magufuli to fear the international community. It is a way of avoiding critical questions regarding his past and present criminal records. He is not ready to face international pressure on matters involving his government in extra-judicial killings, tortures and disappearances of some of his critics, or attempted assassination of political opponents, activists and journalists. It is understood that he has ordered his cabinet ministers to avoid responding to media questions regarding these incidents.

His questionable PhD denies him the integrity and confidence that he wants to associate with his leadership. It is public knowledge that he obtained his PhD from the University of Dar es Salaam as a part-time student in just three years (2006-2009); but the university has no three-year curriculum for a part-time Phd student. He should have done it for at least six years. But when activist Ben Saanane raised queries about the veracity of the president's doctorate in 2016, suggesting Magufuli might have corrupted systems to award him the PhD, he was threatened by unknown people. Shortly after, he went missing.

Sources say Saanane was abducted by Magufuli's "unknown people" who kept the young man in torture chambers for one year before they killed him by feeding him to crocodiles in Ruvu river in late 2017. After Saanane's abduction, Magufuli appointed his doctoral supervisor Prof. Joseph Buchweishaija to the position of permanent secretary. This and other criminal incidents of this nature still haunt Magufuli. He would do whatever it takes to avoid exposure to western media.

Under Magufuli, Tanzania's diplomatic policy is unclear. His iron-fist rule coupled with diplomatic incompetence and uncertainty has eroded gains that Tanzania used to enjoy under presidents Benjamin Mkapa and Jakaya Kikwete - both renowned diplomats - whose presidency had put their country on a clear and respectable diplomatic map.

SAUTI KUBWA - www.sautikubwa.org - an independent website that analyses Tanzania's socio-political affairs, puts it briefly and succinctly in early 2019:

> *"In early November 2018, the EU ambassador to Tanzania was forced to pack and return to Brussels after an endless diplomatic row. The episode was later followed by the EU and US senate publicly expressing deep concerns about deteriorating human rights conditions in Tanzania. The World Bank and various individual donor countries have*

withdrawn their financial support, citing a number of human rights violations.

"President Magufuli has never travelled abroad to address any major international conference since he came to power in 2015. In fact, within diplomatic circles, there is a 'silent debate' on what Tanzania stands for in today's foreign policy. For three years since 2015, there has been a sharp and sudden shift from Tanzania as a perennially vocal liberator and advocate for the rights of the oppressed worldover, to a silent giant in the midst of oppression and tyranny within and without her borders.

"A strong voice that incessantly and successfully fought to liberate several African countries (from colonialism, dictatorship and Apartheid) is currently waning. A relentlessly tireless advocate for the global dignity of humanity has been recently missing out on a global diplomatic forum. What went wrong?

"One senior civil servant anonymously explains: 'Throughout history, our policy has been clear. We always spoke up against atrocity, dictatorship, oppression and even sham elections in other countries. But now, when a lot of such vices is happening around us, unfortunately, no one in the world hears our voice. We are becoming a forgotten voice, and we have unofficially opted to have a cold shoulder on matters of regional and global interest. While Tanzania is abruptly

becoming silent, her regional neighbours seem to be gaining ground. Kenya, one of her main economic competitors, is on the verge of asserting herself as a regional business hub in East Africa.

"Uganda is now relaxing and concentrating on its "natural character" of military adventure. Taking advantage of Tanzania's currently "unclear foreign policy," Rwanda has found an easy ride in her suddenly friendly neighbour. This is a situation that Rwanda had missed in the region for years before 2015.

"Informed voices within the Tanzania's foreign service understand that there have been internal efforts to review the country's foreign policy to fit President Magufuli's political jargon and ambition of "economic diplomacy," but very few of them are optimistic about it. They do not see any strategy to understand and implement it. Nor do they trust his grasp of the concept.

"One former diplomat who served under President Jakaya Kikwete says, again, anonymously for fear of reprisals: 'He (Magufuli) doesn't seem to like diplomacy, in the first place. He is wary of the effects of globalisation, but globalisation is an evil we can't run away from. If we need to attract investments, we must have an enticing and convincing language that builds bridges and connects us with the world. We need a language of business that nurtures our relationships with

international businesses and development partners. As of now, we are lacking this charisma, and our silence is being questioned everywhere.'

"Under Kikwete, whose 10-year tenure ended in 2015, Tanzania was a shining diplomatic icon in the world. He made it his hobby, and he put in place strategies to promote his country abroad. Unfortunately, a regime that came after him seems to be obsessed more with domestic politics than with foreign policy.

"Tanzania has had one of the most qualified foreign ministers – Ambassador Augustine Mahiga. But he seems to have been overwhelmed by his boss's lack of diplomatic taste and, like some of his compatriots put it, he seems to have resigned to himself. He doesn't like any trouble as he approaches retirement."

In fact, a few weeks after the above comments were published on SAUTI KUBWA website, out of this fear and ignorance, accusing his foreign minister of doing soft diplomacy, Magufuli made a mini-reshuffle in which he replaced Ambassador Mahiga with a lawyer, Prof. Palamagamba Kabudi, whose first statement to diplomats was very frustrating and threatening. Kabudi warned diplomats against commenting on Tanzania in a way that would depict it negatively to the world. On the same day he was sworn in as foreign minister, Prof. Kabudi said he would never tolerate critics who expose the government's weaknesses abroad. He said they should either talk about the country's good things or shut up!

This was yet another failure of Magufuli's diplomatic appointments - all because of the fear that engulfs him. In a similar line of English adages, "a guilty conscience needs no accuser," and "the guilty are afraid," Magufuli's sense of fear is definitely an expression of his own guilt in many aspects; and it will not do him, and his country, any good.

HIS FEAR OF HIS CORRUPT PAST

> *"I am resigning because I am sure that if I don't, he will embarrassingly fire me as a retaliation for the story I wrote on how, as cabinet minister, he corruptly awarded a government house to his concubine,"* Muhingo Rweyemamu, former editor and District Commissioner (RIP).

It is not impossible but it is very hard to find a clean politician, especially in a party that has been in power for five decades, more so in African politics. So, while some people might have been led to think Magufuli has been waging war on corruption, and although it is true that he has taken some tough action against some big names, the truth is, there are limits he can go. He may not have deep roots in the political system of his party, but he surely has deep roots in the corrupt regimes of his two predecessors - Benjamin Mkapa and Jakaya Kikwete.

Magufuli's ministerial service never went untainted with corruption. He just had a luck for not being openly implicated in corruption, for two reasons. One, his hard working spirit outweighed his corrupt lifestyle when compared to his fellow ministers. He was known for taking action against lazy subordinates by naming and shaming them. Although this approach has its negative side, the positive one outshone the other part and made him more visible and laudable.

Two, most politicians who were accused of corruption had been involved in a kind of power struggle aiming at running for president. Magufuli never showed any signs of yearning for presidency. Even at the beginning of 2005 when Kikwete and his team were scanning for possible competitors, a senior editor was planted to interview him and ask if he was considering to seek his for his party's nomination. Magufuli said: "No, I am not interested. If it is a matter of presidency, I am a president of roads." By then he had worked as deputy minister for works for five years and as full minister for five years in the same ministry. He was one of Mkapa's most endeared ministers.

This position saved him from Kikwete's ferocious propaganda machinery that used to character assassinate whoever seemed to be standing in the way of Kikwete's presidential interests. No one but Magufuli himself can tell for sure whether or not he harboured any interests for the country's top most job ten years before he assumed it.

His low profile - and probably his hidden interests in the presidency - became a ladder on which he would climb toward grand corruption without being highly noticed or exposed. In 2006, he was implicated in a corrupt deal involving the sale of more than 8,000 residential houses for civil servants.

As minister for works, Magufuli unlawfully usurped powers of chairperson for the Tanzania Building Agency (TBA) and forcefully allocated some of these houses to his younger brother Musa Magufuli, his nephew Dotto James, and his concubine Sundi Malomo. All of them were not civil servants but a way was found to justify this deal. Musa was granted a three-month working contract in the works ministry, and he was given a house in his first month. In his second month, he quit his job. James was fixed somewhere within a roads construction agency from where his uncle later appointed him moved him to finance ministry when he became president. This story was reported by RAI newspaper in 2006, and his decision was reversed later by the lands, housing and human settlements ministry.

In another corrupt incident, when he became minister for lands, housing and human settlements, Magufuli ordered the construction of Rose Garden Bar on a road reserve against established laws, even after Municipal authorities in Kinondoni had revoked the bar owner's title deed for plot number 951. Again, RAI newspaper ran this story in its edition of March 1-7, 2007. Magufuli never forgave the newspaper editors who did the investigation and published the stories.

Coincidentally, Salva Rweyemamu, who had interviewed him about his presidential ambitions, happened to be managing editor of Habari Corporation, a media company that owned and published RAI newspaper. The same person later became director of communications at state house under President Kikwete.

When Magufuli became president, he fired Rweyemamu within his first few days.

The other editor who had reported about the corrupt sale of government houses, Muhingo Rweyemamu, later became a district commissioner under Kikwete. At the time of Magufuli becoming president, Rweyemamu was a District Commissioner in Morogoro. He quit his job voluntarily citing health reasons. Yes, he was having poor health, but shortly before he resigned he spoke to me and said: "I am resigning because I am sure that if I don't, he will embarrassingly fire me as a retaliation for the story I wrote on how, as cabinet minister, he corruptly awarded a government house to his concubine."

On top of that, a good number of official reports by the Controller and Auditor General (CAG) and the Public Procurement Regulatory Authority (PPRA) put Magufuli's integrity on the line.

As minister, he made impulsive orders that caused the government loss of billions of shillings. In one instance, he unlawfully used ministerial powers as fishing minister, and apprehended a fishing boat owned by Chinese nationals in the Indian Ocean. He lost the case and the government was ordered to pay damages worth **1.3 trillion** Tanzanian shillings.

A PPRA report said Magufuli had impulsively halted payment of 124 billion shillings to road contractors, later accumulating huge interests to the tune of 5.3 trillion shillings. On top of that, the PPRA report faulted Magufuli's works ministry for paying 951.7 billion shillings to ghost contractors.

In 2013, the CAG report raised a query about 253 billion shillings that had vanished into thin air under his custody as works minister. During the same period, Magufuli purchased a boat (Mv Bagamoyo) at a very exorbitant price of 8 billion shillings. The CAG said the ministry had purchased a second-hand boat against contractual specification for a new one.

The opposition smelt corruption in the deal and, as they predicted, the ferry developed mechanical failures after making just a single trip to Bagamoyo on 27th February 2015. That was the end of Mv Bagamoyo. It never functioned again. When the noises became louder, Magufuli found a way to silence critics. He donated the ferry to the army. Todate, no one asks about it. A 2016 report by the CAG says the procurement of the boat did not meet requisite specifications and standards, and the ferry's speed did not comply with requirements of the purchaser.

So, it was no big surprise when later as president he ordered the purchase of aircrafts without following laid down laws and budgetary procedures. No wonder in his first budget as president (2016/17) Magufuli fumbled to clear himself of the embarrassment of the apparent loss of 1.5 trillion shillings pointed out by the CAG. The Public Accounts Committee (PAC), having read the annual report of the Controller and Auditor General (CAG) for the year 2016/17, discovered that 1.5 trillion shillings ($640m) was missing. The government did not have any reasonable explanation. So, the parliament ordered a re-audit of the same. The audit report was presented in February 2019, revealing further anomalies. This time the missing funds were not 1.5 trillion shillings, but 2.4 trillion shillings ($1.03bn).

A hefty amount of 976.96 billion shillings was said to have been spent by the State House without parliamentary budget or approval by CAG. The ministry of finance is using the state house as a scapegoat because Vote 20 under which these funds were purportedly reallocated to the State House is never audited. By all standards, this is corruption.

The latest audit report by the Controller and Auditor General (CAG) reveals that during the year 2017/2018, the Magufuli government squandered trillions of shillings through dubious deals and transactions, including illegal procurements and misappropriation through the country's treasury.

In total, 1.3 trillion shillings (equivalent to $562 million, was "embezzled." Out of this amount, the treasury faces an audit query amounting to Tsh 885 billion (equivalent to $382.7m). 432.7 billion shillings, equivalent to $188m, was embezzled through procurement of goods and services from five entities whose suppliers were neither approved nor legally registered.

This is not the first time the CAG's report queries the treasury over misappropriation of public funds. Last year, the audit raised the same query over 751 billion shillings (equivalent to $324.6m) embezzled in the year 2016/2017.

The CAG writes emphatically about this: "I reiterate my prior year recommendation, and (I am) advising accounting officers to keep refraining from diversion of funds, and adhere to expenditures that only fall within the approved budget and the Government Financial Statistics (GFS) codes. Whenever such diversion is inevitable and in line with authority, reallocation warrant has to be sought in conjunction with Section 41 of the Budget Act No. 11 of 2015."

It is understood that some procurement is executed by direct orders from the president, whose nephew, Dotto James, permanent secretary for the ministry of finance, is the treasurer general.

On several occasions, Magufuli has said publicly that he personally ordered the purchase of air eight crafts on advice from Rwanda's President Paul Kagame, against budgetary approval. A few months ago, he said in a public address that the air crafts, managed by Air Tanzania Corporation Limited (ATCL), had made huge financial profits.

But reports reveal that for the past three years, ATCL has incurred massive losses. In 2014/15, the losses amounted to Tsh 94.3 billion. In 2015/16, it made losses to the tune of Tsh 109.2 billion, while in 2017/18, the losses were Tsh 113.7 billion.

Reacting to incessant audit queries, and in effort to avoid further audit, the government is now rearranging the government procurement unit, putting it in the president's office. Sources say the move is being executed following "orders from above," but it will definitely cause further embarrassment and bring about more scandals against the president as he becomes the "procurer-in-chief."

Magufuli enjoys working without being monitored or audited; and he hates criticism of any kind. This attitude explains his government's brutality and hostility against critical media, opposition parties, objective academic researches, and strongly opinionated civil leaders. His most recent action was block publication of an annual report by IMF on the state of the economy in Tanzania; although later the Magufuli's government denied taking such action.

Against this background, it is easy to understand why he ordered the construction of an airport in Chato, his home district, with a budget that had not been allocated by the parliament. This also explains why he decided to purchase planes without involving the cabinet or parliament.

He has no regard to rule of law and accountability. This is how he caused an international uproar when a British construction company seized Tanzania's Q400 Bombardier plane in Canada in 2017 seeking to recover millions of dollars the country owed it as a result of Magufuli's impulsive cancellation of a road project when he was minister. An opposition member of parliament who exposed the seizure later survived an assassination attempt miraculously.

Magufuli' corrupt past still haunts him, and he is afraid of it. He is fighting the media, the opposition and critics because he wants to keep his impulsive and corrupt past buried in complete oblivion. Unfortunately, his tactics seem to be working against his wishes because his past lives with him as president.

HIS FEAR OF HIMSELF

He has portrayed a character of leadership that his people are likely to dislike and fear. He understands there is a barrage of tough questions he is not ready to face. Cowardice holds and drives him.

Besides a corrupt-and-past Magufuli, there is also a present Magufuli - one who has promised, disappointed, maimed, and killed those he is wary of. His schizophrenic syndrome makes him fear himself, thinking that if he changed into a better person, he would have to face himself.

Of all fears that have existed in his government, Magufuli's fear of himself is probably the most deadly one. It makes him live with uncertainty, and it has put his family members on constant stress and anxiety. This fear is based on two insidious mental health manifestations.

The first is his historic hysterical syndrome caused by emotional instability. When this happened in the past, Magufuli sadistically committed some horrible acts against some people. In one episode, it is cited as having negatively affected him in his childhood dream of becoming a Roman Catholic priest, when he mercilessly cut his classmate with a sharp razor blade following a brief argument and misunderstanding between them in a dormitory. That event terrorised his fellow students, and it left evidence for his terrorism against his future compatriots.

In one of his recent speeches before Roman Catholic bishops in April 2019, he reminded them how he had wished to become a bishop. It is probably the same syndrome that had led to him to say in public, in May 2018, that he would wish to become "a leader of angels" when he dies! In 2016, exasperated by what he had termed as indecisiveness of some police officers, he said (in his broken English), "I wish could be IGP" - meaning he would have taken action against them if he had been the Inspector General of Police. This was a bizarre statement from someone who is the IGP's boss! In the same obsession for leadership and recognition, Magufuli told some of his assistants in 2018, when his government was colliding with bishops over its human rights violations, that he wanted church leaders to shut up and acknowledge that "there is only one president." He was apparently ridiculing and belittling the president of the Tanzania Episcopal Conference.

In November 2016, his wife was briefly admitted at the Muhimbili National Hospital for an unknown illness, but some of his aides claimed she had been a victim of physical assault by her husband following a verbal exchange between the first couple - in the presence of some of their assistants. Even as minister, Magufuli was known for terrorising and even beating up some of his family members.

He is not in the best books of some of his uncles in Chato following endless disagreements over some family matters, including land acquisition. Some of them even narrate a past horrible incident of Magufuli ending an argument with his uncles by dismantling a coffin they had prepared for his father's burial, insisting they should use the coffin he had purchased.

As president, with all security forces around him, he has become a perfect bully from whose wrath many people seek to distance themselves. Without remorse, Magufuli has continued to capitalise on his intolerance and short tamper to create more victims and more enemies.

The second manifestation of his mental condition that creates fear of himself, is his chronic abusive behaviour towards his subordinates, particularly women. This behaviour cuts across his entire career. A long list of his victims includes watchmen, drivers, secretaries, his children, his wife, his sisters, his uncles, and his business partners. His abusive inclination ranges from physical abuse and torture, psychological torture, public ridicule, insensitive and demeaning language towards women, including his vice president and one former female diplomat.

In 2016, he fired Wilson Kabwe, a senior government official, at a public rally in Dar es Salaam, ignoring all labour and employment laws. Kabwe had been implicated with some scandals in his position as city director. Attending the same rally, Makonda, one of Magufuli's corrupt buddies and cronies, had just accused Kabwe of engaging in corrupt practices in some city projects. He pleaded for the president's action. In immediate response, Magufuli asked masses attending his rally: "Should I fire him?" "Yeees," the people roarred in response, perhaps taking it less seriously. He fired Kabwe instantly. The fired official developed sudden stress and depression. He died a few weeks later.

With this background in the public domain, Magufuli fears any unfortunate moment that would lead to anyone - particularly his victims - exposing and embarrassing him and the presidency. He lives with this fear around his neck.

In 2015, during the early days of presidential aspirants in his party as he sought nomination, a group of concerned individuals sought audience with eminent people in the party to warn against the danger of Magufuli becoming a president. They solely zeroed in on his mental condition, categorically saying he was incapable of handling the presidency. This group of concerned people included his former school mates, fellow teachers and engineers, relatives and former girlfriends. At one point, they sought opinion from his wife. She neither declined nor affirmed their characterisation of her husband.

This news spread to the intelligence service. A senior intelligence officer was dispatched to dig deeper into these allegations. He later said, "there was no way Magufuli can be entrusted with the management of our country." Magufuli has tried many times to seek remedy through religious experiences, traditional healers and conventional medicine. In effort to psychologically dissociate himself from this condition, to shield it from public eyes, he ends up creating internal fear of himself, and he projects the same to others by terrorising them.

Above all, Magufuli fears his own failures particularly his flops in human rights and economy. Out of ignorance and arrogance, he has put more emphasis on prohibitive taxation and has undermined tax incentives, political freedom, economic freedom, and individual civil liberties. Under his leadership, the private sector has suffered the worst consequences as he attempts to build an economy that is completely controlled by his government, ignoring the forces of globalisation, trade and investment.

The country's economic growth is retarding. In 2019, IMF reported it at 4 percent, down from 7 percent that had been projected by the government. Few, if any jobs, have been created. His government has reneged on annual increments for, and promotion of, civil servants. His industrialisation agenda remains a disappointment to both himself and the people. It is a mere political rhetoric that some critics have called "a long journey with no clear destination." Life has not been easier for common people.

In 2016, when his government embarked on a strategy to address scarcity of sugar supply in the country, it ordered retailers to sell a kilo of sugar at 1,800 shillings. About 300,000 hectares of land were earmarked for sugarcane plantations. The project would have resulted in producing 1.5 million tonnes of sugar with its multiplier effects in terms of foreign currency, generation of employment, etc. Nothing meaningful happened. As a result, the price of a kilo of sugar hiked from 1,800 shillings to 3,000 shillings in just three years.

In 2016, his government came up with an idea to produce a large quantity of edible oil seeds particularly for sunflowers and palm trees. Singida, Manyara, Dodoma and Kigoma regions were earmarked for this investment. In Kigoma alone, 200,000 hectares were allocated from which 800,000 tonnes of raw palm oil would be produced. Eight factories were to be constructed for processing palm oil. By 2018, only 180,000 tonnes of edible oils had been produced, being 30 percent of domestic needs (400,000 -520,000 tonnes annually). As a result, the price for a 20-litre bucket of edible oils shot up from 55,000 shillings in 2016 to 70,000 shillings in 2018.

In another attempt, in 2016, the government promised in parliament to construct several textile industries so as to add value to locally produced cotton and to revamp the peasants' economy. This strategy was meant to create jobs and enable Tanzania to export clothes instead of raw cotton. Three years down the line, nothing materialised - no industries, no jobs, no export of clothes. Tanzania still imports clothes. Due to his bad economic management, many businesses including tourist lodges, hotels, banks and forex bureaus were badly affected and closed, as a number of major projects, including road construction, were halted in 2019 - killing capital and jobs, and plunging more people into financial hardships.

His government lacks discipline in handling budgetary allocations. In 2016/17, for instance, some sensitive ministries were heavily underfunded, receiving funds ranging from 2 to 11 percents of the the allocated budget. The biggest chunks, over 300 percent of budgeted funds, were silently diverted to the president's office and police. In 2016/2017, the ministry of agriculture received only two percent of the amount that had been allocated by parliament (100.527 billion shillings); while in 2017/2018 the same ministry received 11 percent of the total funds (150.253 billion shillings).

In 2016, the parliament allocated 4 billion shillings for the ministry of livestock and fisheries. The government released only 130 million shillings, equivalent to 3.25 percent of the total budget. In 2017/2018, out of 4 billion shillings allocated by parliament for the same ministry, no single shilling had been released as of March 2018, according to the controller and auditor general's report.

So, Magufuli's empty promises to common people have become his own burden, and a thorn in his own flesh. His people's economic situations keep worsening month after month. Despite his resolve to silence the opposition and use state resources for his political propaganda, his popularity ratings are the lowest ever, having fallen by 41 percent in two years as of July 2018 - from 96 percent in 2016 to 55 percent in 2018.

When he looks at himself, his promises, his deeds and omissions, he knows that the Tanzanian people look at him as a deceitful, insincere, merciless, and brutal leader. Seeking to force everyone to like him and praise him, he has ended up being a tyrant, shutting up whoever speaks openly about his failed leadership.

He has portrayed a character of leadership that his people are likely to dislike and fear. He understands there is a barrage of tough questions he is not ready to face. Cowardice holds him and drives him. With his autocratic efforts he tends to turn his citizens into subjects. He threatens his people because he fears them. He fears them because, as a true despot, he is not at peace with his own character.

HIS FEAR OF THE JUDICIARY

To Magufuli, the judiciary is a small department under his wings. It is alleged that through the chief justice and chief judge, Magufuli has been transferring and appointing judges to undertake special court cases. A senior magistrate who unconstitutionally denied bail to the leader of official opposition and a female member of parliament in 2018, leading them to spend 104 days in remand prison, was promoted to high court judge even before his ruling was eventually overturned by the court of appeal.

Magufuli's fear of the judiciary is open and obvious. His career, both as minister, member of parliament and president, is tainted with serious disregard of law and order. Even his nickname "bulldozer" comes from his obsession with lawlessness. Without remorse, he has destroyed people's properties, crops, animals, businesses and lives. It is not a surprise, therefore, that his government is equally tainted with the worst human rights violation records since independence.

Since he came to power, he has had his critics abducted, tortured, maimed, harassed, killed, assassinated, held in remand prison without trial and having their property confiscated without due procedures. In just three years, over 16,000 businesses closed down (as per parliamentary speech by finance minister), others declared bankruptcy, with some government law enforcement agents stealing and robbing from people in broad daylight. With this record, Magufuli has every reason to fear the rule of law and, thus, the judiciary.

When he assumed presidency in 2015, the judiciary, which is supposed to be one of the most independent arms of the state, was under the leadership of Chief Justice Mohamed Chande Othman. Despite the offer from Magufuli to extend his term after reaching a retirement age, Justice Othman declined and went into retirement.

Magufuli then unconstitutionally appointed Prof. Ibrahim Juma as "Acting" Chief Justice. When the opposition questioned this irregularity, he confirmed him to the position. Senior judges were irritated by this move, and some of them alleged secretly that Magufuli was, behind the curtain, making agreement with the Chief Justice to silently influence the judiciary in supporting the government's position in human rights violations. These allegations were partly confirmed when Magufuli openly gave an offer to the judiciary on the 2016 Law Day, saying he was willing to offer all penalties collected by the court if the judiciary sped up the process and ruled all pending cases in favour of the government.

It is common knowledge that government underfunding of judiciary in Tanzania is one of its major constraints, a means used to handicap the rule of law. Prior to this statement, the Chief Justice had just made a public plea asking the government to increase funding to the judiciary. Magufuli took advantage of the situation to propose an "open bribery" to the judiciary.

Besides, Magufuli is notorious for interfering with the judicial process. Through his secret service, he has been tagging judges' phones, intimidating them through intelligence service, denying them rights to medical care and family time. At one time, he openly disclosed how he was even following them while they were travelling outside the country. Against existing laws and the constitution, he is forcing judges to obtain his permission before travelling abroad, even on vacation. Obviously, this habit violates judicial independence.

In one of his recent regional tours in Southern Tanzania, he publicly ordered the promotion of a magistrate to high court judge. This is both unconstitutional and unprocedural, and such a judge cannot be expected to dispense justice. Above all, Magufuli has been making questionable appointments of judges, leaving a lot of doubts on the quality and independence of the appointed officials.

To Magufuli, the judiciary is a small department under his wings. It is alleged that through the chief justice and chief judge, Magufuli has been transferring and appointing judges to undertake special court cases. A senior magistrate who unconstitutionally denied bail to the leader of official opposition and a female member of parliament in 2018, leading them to spend 104 days in remand prison, was promoted to high court judge even before his ruling was eventually overturned by the court of appeal.

Under Magufuli, both police and intelligence service are holding people for months without trial, and the judiciary, at most, remains silent. Magufuli fears an independent judiciary because it would overturn his impunity and unconstitutionality.

Tanzania is currently facing at least 14 litigations in international tribunals due to his government's breach of contracts and agreements. There is a growing concern in the the legal fraternity, involving sitting judges and retired ones, about Magufuli's inclination for messing up with the judiciary. It is common knowledge to most of them how similar dictators, particularly in Idi Amin's Uganda and Daniel arap Moi's Kenya, maltreated independent judges. At least there is evidence that one court ruling that sent an opposition parliamentarian for Mbeya Urban to prison, was drafted in the ruling party office, and it was only delivered to the magistrate.

Censoring rulings written by judges is another threat that worries judges, magistrates and legal counsels. Some of judges have been asked, either by the chief justice or by chief judge, to be sending drafts of the rulings before delivering them in court. On one occasion, at a court session in Arusha, a magistrate had to revoke his own ruling on granting a bail just a few minutes after he had granted it. There was some political pressure and life threats on his neck. He revoked it and disappeared for weeks.

The undue pressure on the judges is increasing with fictitious allegations of corruption against some of those who crave and advocate for the independence of the judiciary. Some of the judges have been secretly harassed by Magufuli's special security unit, and have been interrogated by the anti-corruption squad. In just three years, three judges opted to resign to avoid being implicated with complicity of the judiciary into the executive branch.

The constitution stipulates that, if there are corruption allegations against judges, the president shall appoint a three judge panel from Commonwealth countries to carry out an investigation. No commission has been appointed so far for sitting or resigned judges and, thus, Magufuli is using undue pressure to intimidate them.

His fear of the judiciary went to the extreme in 2017 when the Tanganyika Law Society (TLS) openly opposed his disregard for rule of law, and it opted to elect as president one of his fiercest critics, Tundu Lissu. The Minister for Legal and Constitutional Affairs, Dr. Harrison Mwakyembe, accused TLS of engaging in political activism, saying the government would deregister the bar association if the lawyers elected Lissu. He was greeted with a barrage of criticism from various corners of the legal fraternity in Tanzania and beyond. The lawyers stuck to their guns, ignored the government's empty threats and elected Lissu in March 2017. Six months later, after suffering and surviving a series of arbitrary arrests, Lissu was gunshot by "unknown people."

In the TLS elections that followed - in 2018 and 2019 - the government exerted similar efforts and threats to deter lawyers from choosing Fatma Karume and Rugemeleza Nshala, respectively, but it lost the battle because of the lawyers' determination to defend their integrity and professionalism against the government's undue influence. But it never ended without the government sabotaging Ms Karume by preventing her from attending the 2018 Law Day, celebrated at the State House in Dar es Salaam, where she was expected to deliver her TLS speech. Magufuli was the celebration's chief guest. She eventually opted to publish the speech online.

Generally, out of fear, Magufuli is tampering with independence of the judiciary to protect his corrupt leadership and avoid humiliation but, despite elements of timidity and complicity among certain officials, this pillar of the state still enjoys some levels of independence and integrity hardly found in the executive or the legislature. At least, the judiciary is helping to expose the despot's cowardice, keeping him worried and terrified.

ABOUT THE AUTHOR

Ansbert Ngurumo is a philosopher and award-winning journalist; a human rights defender, a political analyst and newspaper editor. His journalism experience spans over 20 years. Having worked with several media houses, he is a former managing editor of two mainstream newspapers in Tanzania – *Tanzania Daima* and *MwanaHALISI*. Ngurumo has an academic background in literature, systematic philosophy, journalism and business management; and has mainly written for various media outlets in Tanzania, Kenya, and South Africa on politics, business, human rights, health, and education.

A former chief media adviser to opposition presidential candidate in Tanzania (2010), Ngurumo is a founder, editor and publisher of **www.sautikubwa.org** - a pro-democracy website established in April 2018 to counter the wave of authoritarian rule, and to publish "forbidden news" as the Magufuli regime has been struggling to suppress freedom of thought. Besides journalism, Ngurumo has also been a choir trainer and choral music composer since 1985. He is a political columnist and commentator, a leader, a blogger, a translator, and a fundraiser. He has previously translated two religious books on *God's Mercy* - *"Jesus I Trust in You!"* and *"God, Rich in Mercy*!" - from English to Kiswahili, and he recently published an e-book *"Reflections of a seasoned journalist."* He is one of hundreds of victims of Magufuli's autocracy. Luckily, he survived an abduction incident in October 2017, eventually ending up in exile in Europe. He remains connected and informed about crucial matters in, and about, Tanzania.

23534586R00087

Printed in Great Britain
by Amazon